'None was closer to the cross of Christ than the two criminals crucified either side of him. Graham Reeves invites us to reflect on their contrasting responses as these malefactors turn to the one condemned as they are. Here is an inspirational study, informed by the author's wide reading and extensive pastoral experience. Graham Reeves has the rare gift of making new connections. In *Two Other Men* he deploys that gift brilliantly. With each new connection a switch is thrown and fresh light breaks from the all too familiar story – a light to lighten our darkness too.'
Dr John Pridmore, former Rector of Hackney

'Which of the two thieves are you? Through self-examination we learn to discern the good and the bad within us. Graham Reeves has written an interesting and informative work to help us on our spiritual journeys.'
The Right Reverend Abbot Giles Hill OSB, Abbot of Our Lady and St John Abbey, Alton

G000065933

Two Other Men

Lessons from the thieves in the crucifixion narrative of St Luke

GRAHAM REEVES

instant
apostle

First published in Great Britain in 2017

Instant Apostle
The Barn
1 Watford House Lane
Watford
Herts
WD17 1BJ

British Library Cataloguing-in-Publication Data

A catalogue record for this book is available from the British Library

This book and all other Instant Apostle books are available from Instant Apostle:

Website: www.instantapostle.com

E-mail: info@instantapostle.com

ISBN 978-1-909728-59-2

Printed in Great Britain

This book is dedicated to the memory of
John, Delma, Malcolm and Alison.
'Today you will be with me in Paradise.'

Contents

Acknowledgements

The idea for this book came as a result of a request to lead a monastic retreat during Advent in 2011. Some of the material from that retreat has found its way into this book, but much has been added and altered as the topic of the 'thieves' crucified alongside Jesus has occupied my thoughts. I am grateful to the Right Reverend Dom Giles Hill OSB, Abbot of the Benedictine monastery of Our Lady and St John, Alton, Hampshire, and the community of monks for their constant support and prayerful example. I would also like to give thanks to the Reverend Dr John Pridmore whose writings have nourished me for many years, and to Father Frank Smith and John Wetherell who not only remind me in word and deed of the importance of maintaining the faith handed down from the Apostles but are also good friends.

I am also very pleased that my old tutor Dr Ian Boxall, Associate Professor of New Testament at the Catholic University of America, agreed to write a foreword. Now a distinguished scholar of the New Testament, his teaching and writing is bringing the Scriptures to life for a whole new generation.

Others I would like to give thanks to include Mary Wardell for reading and correcting the original manuscript, the Reverend Sarah Manouch, Bradley Smith and all the faithful at St Mary's Barnham in West Sussex, the team at Instant Apostle, John Dudley, a true artisan, and Gareth Scourfield, a friend and author who inspires and radiates life.

Finally, I thank my wife Jackie for her constant support and encouragement, for the laughter and the love, and Alex, a fine young man.

Foreword

Luke's story of the penitent thief at the cross (Luke 23:39-43), like so many scenes shaped by Luke's literary artistry, has had a profound impact on the Christian imagination. Although only five verses in length, this passage continues to appeal to readers owing to its capacity to tap into the complexity of human existence, the stirrings of faith and the struggles of discipleship. Moreover, as Graham Reeves reminds us in this profound reflection, it is not the story of the penitent thief. Rather, it is the story of two thieves, two characters who mirror in different ways our own struggles, longings, commitments and compromises. It is unsurprising, therefore, that in later legendary embellishments of their story, both these unnamed characters are given names. For posterity, at least in Western Christianity, they are remembered as Gestas and Dismas.

Throughout this study, Graham Reeves proves himself a sensitive and trustworthy guide to the many dimensions of this rich Lucan story. He has plumbed its depths, and presents us with the fruits of his grappling with the passage. He has also been sensitive to the broader context of Luke's Gospel, where Luke's pairings of characters often challenges naïve dualistic distinctions. Reeves offers us an imaginative reading of Scripture, interwoven with apocryphal texts, ancient Christian poetry, contemporary authors and liturgy, to enable us to engage with this story at many levels. Most significantly, it is profoundly pastoral, as he draws upon his wealth of experience as a mental health chaplain and as a priest who has spent many hours with those who, like the two thieves, were close to death. Particularly compelling is Reeves' treatment of what this story reveals about the true nature of healing, and its relevance for the church's present-day healing ministry.

Read this book. Better, use this book as material for your own personal retreat. In it Reeves takes us on a journey, not simply into the lives of the two thieves at the cross, but also into our own lives, so as to understand ourselves more deeply. We find ourselves to the right and the left of Jesus: the choice of the two thieves is also our choice. In locating ourselves there, we also learn more deeply about the God who is rich in mercy, a mercy which was such a driving force for the evangelist Luke in composing his Gospel. Ultimately, Reeves' reflections raise this challenging question which cuts across our human desire to divide neatly into right and left, deserving and undeserving, good and bad: in the triumph of God's mercy, can even the so-called impenitent thief ultimately be excluded?

Ian Boxall
Washington, DC

Introduction

Jesus was once asked a question. The question was submitted by a Pharisee described as being an expert in the law:

> But when the Pharisees heard that he had silenced the Sadducees, they came together. And one of them, a lawyer, asked him a question, to test him. 'Teacher, which is the great commandment in the law?' And he said to him, 'You shall love the Lord your God with all your heart, and with all your soul, and with all your mind. This is the great and first commandment. And a second is like it, You shall love your neighbor as yourself. On these two commandments depend all the law and the prophets.'
> *Matthew 22:34-40*

Jesus condenses the Hebrew Scriptures into two sentences and renders the bulk of the same Scriptures as commentary to these two pivotal commands. Acknowledging the centrality of these commandments and acting upon them brings one into very close proximity to the Kingdom of God (Mark 12:28-34).

What if a similar question were to be asked of the Christian Scriptures? What would be a pivotal moment in the Gospel narrative from which one could hang the message and meaning of the life and work of Jesus? How about this:

> One of the criminals who were hanged railed at him, saying, 'Are you not the Christ? Save yourself and us!' But the other rebuked him, saying, 'Do you not fear God, since you are under the same sentence of condemnation? And we indeed justly; for we are receiving the due reward of our deeds; but this man has done nothing wrong.' And he said, 'Jesus, remember me when you come into your kingdom.' And he said to him, 'Truly, I say to you, today you will be with me in Paradise.'
> *Luke 23:39-43*

When we stand at the foot of the cross in awe, wonder and adoration, our senses are overwhelmed by the drama of our salvation being played out. On the wood of the cross hangs the Saviour of the world, and we are very close to the Kingdom of God when we seek to understand what is happening here in this crucible of torture, with a view to transforming our lives and making it count in the lives of others. St Luke gives us a crucial insight into understanding what is happening here, and he does so through the brief but powerful conversation that passes between Jesus and the men nailed to two other crosses.

In the company of Jesus and the two thieves we see a fallen world reflected and a new world glimpsed and promised. We see what we are in our fallen nature with all its distortions and selfish impulses; we see who Jesus is in the fullness of His humanity and divinity; we see what God is doing for us through and in Jesus; and we see what we can become, what awaits and what sweet words will fall upon our ears in the promise of eternity with the Lord.

Within the narrative of St Mark's, St Matthew's and St John's Gospels (Mark 15:27, 32b; Matthew 27:44 and John 19:18), only the fact that Jesus was crucified between two bandits (two 'others' in St John) and that they reviled Him are recorded. Only in St Luke's Gospel is this account of the thieves expanded and treated in a distinctive way. It is therefore safe to suggest that St Luke intends to present to his audience a theological and pastoral message that not only fulfils in real terms the life and ministry of Jesus but also brings to a defining moment what St Luke has been writing about Jesus throughout the entirety of his Gospel.

St Luke, in his close following of the events of the life of Jesus, uses the drama of the crucifixion of the two thieves to tell two stories that parallel our own. The two people either side of Jesus are not much different from us, and within the bigger story that St Luke has been telling up to this point, if we indeed see echoes of our own guiding principles in life, then we are presented with some critical choices.

The choice in question is captured succinctly in the alleged words of St Augustine in one of his reflections: 'Do not despair, one of the thieves was saved; do not presume, one of the thieves was damned.'[1] Generally speaking, most ink spilt over the interpretation of the account of the thieves concentrates on this strict dichotomy between the penitent thief and the impenitent thief; a strict black and white interpretation of acceptance and condemnation which depicts the impenitent thief as a dark, unrelenting and ultimately damned character who stands as the perfect foil to the repentant, enlightened, saved thief.

The characterisation of each of the thieves as either good or bad is reinforced by exegetes, homilists, commentators, church history and storytellers, which leaves us in no doubt that the recipient of God's grace, mercy and saving power is the repentant thief, while the thief fixed to the cross on Jesus' left is quietly forgotten about at best, or is the object of evil personified at worst. That might be rightly so; maybe it is St Luke's intention to stun us out of our waywardness and make some decisive, life-changing promises. But then there is the comment made by the priest and writer John Pridmore in his compilation of reflections on the lectionary for Palm Sunday Year C.[2] He writes:

> Luke's gospel is good news for those who feel bad. His narrative is crowded with characters who are ashamed of themselves … These and others like them, the least deserving and the last you'd expect, discover that they have been loved all along. Last in Luke's long gallery of cameo studies of those who have lost all hope for themselves is the 'penitent thief', crucified alongside Jesus. About to die, he has no time left to put his house in order or to make any reparation to those he has injured. Yet when he asks to be remembered, he is promised paradise. Heaven is promised to the undeserving. That promise is our only hope.
>
> But just a moment. There is someone else there still less deserving … the criminal who doesn't ask to be remembered. What about him?[3]

What about him, indeed? Obviously that is not something that could possibly be known. However, in writing this extended reflection on this particular moment in our Lord's crucifixion, and as we stand at Calvary, stare into the faces of the thieves, look at the dying face of the One pierced for our sins and listen to the loaded words that pass between them, it is hoped that by the end we will have much more to say about both thieves. How will this be achieved?

In the first chapter the aim will be to say a little more about these two people who hang at arm's length and within a confessional whisper of being granted salvation. Drawing on apocryphal texts, meditations and the scriptural words used to label Jesus' companions, a fuller description of the thieves will be attempted which will present them as flesh and blood characters.

Chapter two will look more closely at St Luke's literary technique of presenting throughout the Gospel contrasting pairs – for example, Zechariah and Mary, John the Baptist and Jesus, the Prodigal Son and his brother, Dives and Lazarus, and the Pharisee and the tax collector. When the contrasts have been made, what is it that Luke wants the reader to understand, and ultimately, do they prepare the reader for the final contrasting characters: the thieves?

The third chapter will view the crucifixion of the thieves in the Lucan narrative within the larger context of Luke's Gospel, and ask the question, 'Why does Luke expand the tradition of the death of the thieves?' Is it St Luke's way of finally making clear that Jesus is the Saviour, a title given to Jesus which is typically Lucan? What does St Luke want us to take away from this reading that reinforces all that he has written beforehand? And can the evidence underline our understanding of Luke as the *scriba mansuetudinus Christi*, the scribe of the gentleness of Jesus.

Having established the importance of presenting Jesus as the Saviour, chapter four will endeavour to work within this framework of salvation and ask the question, 'What does the respective "yes" and "no" of each pairing tell the reader to finally expect in the "yes" and "no" of each thief and the consequence of each path of choice in their relationship with God?'

Chapter five will look again at the conversation that passes between Jesus and the thieves and ask if there is something in the words and the motives that helps to understand the theology of healing, the difference between healing and curing, and our own prayers for healing.

In chapter six there will be a closer examination of the configuration of the thieves in relation to Jesus. Is there a theological meaning to the placing of the impenitent thief on Jesus' left and the penitent thief to Jesus' right? And can a theological understanding of these positions provide a parallel with the two most significant religious experiences of the Jewish people, the Exodus and the Exile?

Following on from looking at 'rightness' and 'leftness', chapter seven will be an exercise in the imagination. It will be a speculation on the individual psyches of each of the thieves and Jesus, construed from their conversations. As a framework, the Jungian psychological concept of the 'shadow side' will be applied, and the same questions asked of the thieves will be asked of Jesus. Did Jesus have a shadow side? By asking this question of each person crucified at Golgotha, how can this help in our own inner life and growth?

Chapter eight will cover such topics as the message of the three crosses, the question of the penitent thief in relation to baptism, the right approach to death, what the reader of St Luke's description of the crucifixion can learn about prayer, and how liturgy handles the Lucan text.

Finally, in chapter nine, the question will be posed, 'Is there any possibility of salvation for the impenitent thief?' Is there more we can say about him, or is his eternity a foregone conclusion?

Calvary is a truly ghastly place, a disturbing place. We are standing and watching men being executed – one innocent of all crimes, two receiving what their deeds deserved. Ultimate words are being uttered, loaded words, words that are shaping destinies for the ones saying them and the ones listening to them. If these words are truly heard and the consequences of their meaning are given the utmost importance, then this conversation that takes place on Golgotha is the most important in human history. So what is to be our response? Do we join in the derision, wag our heads and mock? Do we demand miraculous signs and miracles as the only means to believe, as did those who stood and watched, and as so many do today? Or do the scales finally fall from our eyes? Do we allow God to penetrate the thick skin of our own selfishness so that we may see what is truly happening before our eyes? Can we, at the last, stand with Mary the blessed Mother of our Lord, St John, the grieving women, the centurion and the thief who recognised Jesus' kingship, and hear the promise of salvation?

[1] Although these words are attributed to St Augustine, scholars are agreed that they are not in his works and are from a later date. See https://fauxtations.wordpress.com/2015/01/10/st-augustine-despair-presumption/ (accessed 14th November 2016).

[2] Revised Common Lectionary.

[3] John Pridmore, *The Word is Very Near You: A Guide to Preaching the Lectionary, Year C* (Norwich: Canterbury Press, 2009), p.120.

Chapter 1
Who were the thieves?

Who were the two people who shared that horrific fate on that rubbish tip outside the walls of Jerusalem? The honest answer is, 'We don't know.' What we do know is that Jesus wasn't crucified on His own that first Good Friday, and that Scripture describes them by their misdeeds.

Both St Mark (15:27) and St Matthew (27:38) describe the two either side of Jesus as *lestai*, translated as robbers, bandits or revolutionaries. St John (19:18) describes the two as simply *duo allous* – two others. St Luke, on the other hand, while using the word *lestai* to describe the group that attacked the traveller in the parable of the Good Samaritan (Luke 10:30), uses the word *kakourgos*, meaning criminal, malefactor, in relation to the thieves (Luke 23:32).

It seems that St Luke deliberately avoids the word *lestai* to distance himself from the label of 'revolutionary' (cf. Luke 22:52), for St John describes Barabbas in the same way (John 18:30), and as Pope Benedict XVI points out:

> They are regarded as resistance fighters, to whom the Romans, in order to criminalise them, simply attach the word 'robber' … The offense attributed to Jesus though is of a different kind from that of the two robbers, who may have taken part in Barabbas' uprising. Pilate is well aware that Jesus had nothing like that in mind, and

so he adopts a particular formulation of Jesus' 'crime' in the charge that is placed above the Cross: 'Jesus of Nazareth, King of the Jews' (John 19:19).[4]

Taking a step back for the moment, the crucifixion of Jesus amid the robbers is the fulfilment of Isaiah's prophecy in the Suffering Servant passages of Isaiah 53. Familiar to many from the liturgical readings of Holy Week, we hear in verse 12 of chapter 53:

> Therefore I will divide him a portion with the great,
> and he shall divide the spoil with the strong;
> because he poured out his soul to death,
> and was numbered with the transgressors;
> yet he bore the sin of many,
> and made intercession for the transgressors.

The detailed description that St Luke gives of the crucifixion events evidences his own programme of making 'a narrative of the things which have been accomplished among us' (Luke 1:1). No reading of Isaiah 53 could leave one in doubt that the reality of Jesus' Passion breaks open the prophet's words into something comprehensible, unless of course, like the disciples on the road to Emmaus (Luke 24), a 'foolish and slow heart' prevents seeing what the prophets were pointing towards all along. The culmination of Isaiah's vision in 53:12 is nothing less than St Luke's account, the only difference being that the prophetic voice becomes the event that becomes certain (Luke 1:4), evidentially true (Luke 1:2) and tradition (Luke 1:2).

The reader is left in no doubt that Jesus was not on His own at Golgotha, and that the company flanking His right and His left were men of disreputable character and suspect morals who were deserving of the punishment being meted out. This was even admitted by the thief on Jesus' right who recognised their sentence as being just. What more can we say about them?

In 'fact', that is about as far as we can go, but when 'facts' end, 'myth' takes over. For in a need to satiate a curiosity of what the Gospels and Epistles are silent about, Christians in the second and third centuries began to write up their own, often sensational stories that were deemed unworthy as ecclesial, orthodox documents for the spiritual growth of the faithful. Given the term 'apocryphal', these secondary texts, often termed 'Gospel', 'Acts', 'Epistle' and 'Apocalypse', occasionally tell fantastic stories that centre on the birth of Jesus and His childhood, the ministry of Jesus, His death, heaven and hell, and individual people such as Mary and Joseph, Pilate, Veronica, Paul and the other disciples.

For the purposes of this book, four apocryphal texts, a letter of St Anselm and a meditation of Blessed Anne Catherine Emmerich give details of the thieves. In each case it is worth noting the lengths to which the writers go in their handling of the respective thieves to make a clear theological point when reading the apocryphal material back into the canonical Lucan account. These texts are, The Arabic Infancy Gospel, The Gospel of Peter, The Narrative of Joseph of Arimathaea, The Apocryphal Gospel of Nicodemus, St Anselm's meditation on the childhood of Jesus, and Blessed Anne Catherine Emmerich's The Dolorous Passion of Our Lord Jesus Christ.

The Arabic Infancy Gospel, v23

And departing from this place, they came to a desert; and hearing that it was infested with robbers, Joseph and the Lady Mary decided to cross this region by night. But on their way, behold, they saw two robbers lying in wait on the road, and with them a great number of robbers who were their associates, sleeping. Now these two robbers into whose hands they had fallen were Titus and Dumachus. Titus therefore said to Dumachus, 'I beseech you to let these persons go free, so that our comrades do not see them.' And as Dumachus refused, Titus said to him again, 'Take forty drachmas from me, and have them as a pledge.' At the same time he held out to him the belt which he had had about his waist, that he should not open his mouth or speak. And the Lady Mary, seeing that the robber had done them a kindness, said to him, 'The Lord God will sustain you with his right hand, and will grant you remission of your sins.' And the Lord Jesus answered and said to his mother, 'Thirty years hence, O my mother, the Jews will crucify me at Jerusalem, and these two robbers will be raised upon the cross along with me, Titus on my right hand and Dumachus on my left; and after that day Titus will go before me into Paradise.' And she said, 'God keep this from you my son.' And they went from there toward a city of idols, which, when they came near it, was transformed into sand-hills.[5]

The Gospel of Peter, v10-14

And they brought two malefactors and crucified the Lord between them. But he held his peace as he felt no pain. And when they had set up the cross, they wrote, THIS IS THE KING OF ISRAEL. And having laid down his garments before him, they divided them among themselves and cast lots for them. But one of the malefactors rebuked them saying; 'we are suffering for the deeds we have committed; but this man who has become the saviour of men, what wrong has he done you?' And they were angry with him, and commanded that his legs should not be broken so that he might die in torment.[6]

The Narrative of Joseph of Arimathea, chapter 1

In those days in which they condemned the Son of God to be crucified, seven days before Christ suffered, two condemned robbers were sent from Jericho to procurator Pilate; and their case was as follows. The first, his name Gestas, put travellers to death murdering them with the sword and others he exposed naked. And he hung up women by their heels, head down, and cut off their breasts and drank the blood of infants limbs, never having known God, not obeying laws, being violent from the beginning, and doing such deeds.

And the case of the other was as follows. He was called Demas and was by birth a Galilean and kept an inn. He made attacks upon the rich, but was good to the poor, a thief like Tobit, for he buried the bodies of the poor.

The narrative then goes on to describe in detail the conversation between Jesus and the thieves:

> And they were nailed up along with Jesus, Gestas on the left and Demas on the right.
>
> And the man on the left began to cry out, and said to Jesus: 'see how many evil deeds I did on earth. If I had known you were a King, I would have destroyed you too.'... But the robber on the right hand whose name was Demas saw the Godlike grace of Jesus and said, 'I know you are the Son of God. I see you, Christ, adored by countless of angels. Pardon me my sins ...'
>
> And when the robber had said these things, Jesus said to him: 'Truly I say to you, Demas that today you shall be with me in Paradise'... And he said to the robber: 'Go and speak to the Cherubim and the powers who wield the flaming sword, who have guarded Paradise from the time that Adam, the first creation, was in Paradise .... Until I come the second time to judge living and the dead. ... I require and order that he who has been crucified along with me should go enter, and receive remission of sins through me, and that, having put on an incorruptible body, he should go into Paradise and dwell where nobody has been able to dwell.'[7]

The Gospel of Nicodemus, 7:1, 3, 10-13

> Then Jesus went out of the hall and the two thieves with him ... And in like manner did they to the two thieves who were crucified with him, Dismas on the right hand, and Gestas on his left ...

But one of the two thieves who were crucified with Jesus, whose name was Gestas, said to Jesus, if thou art the Christ, deliver thyself and us.

But the thief who was crucified on his right hand, whose name was Dismas, answering, rebuked him, and said, Dost not thou fear God, who art condemned to this punishment? We indeed receive rightly and justly the demerit of our actions; but this Jesus, what evil hath he done?

After this groaning, he said to Jesus, Lord, remember me when thou comest into thy Kingdom.

Jesus answering said to him, Verily I say unto thee, that this day thou shalt be with me in Paradise.[8]

St Anselm: Meditation on the Childhood of Jesus

It was the time of the massacre of the holy innocents. St Joseph, Our Lady and the Divine Infant were fleeing from Herod. Leaving Bethlehem, the Holy Family entered the land of Egypt which sacred scriptures calls the country of sin where God had withdrawn from his people, a country that only the sacrifice of Christ could redeem. On this flight into the country of the devil, Jesus, Mary and Joseph entered a forest inhabited by brigands. Among them was Dismas, a murderer and a thief. However, in the depths of his soul lay some secret graces he had not refused. Hidden from sight, waiting for an unsuspecting victim, Dismas saw the approach of a man and a young woman carrying a child. The three travellers had some baggage, perhaps some of the gifts of the Magi Kings reserved for the long trip. Dismas judged that this unprotected caravan would not offer resistance. The staff of St Joseph caused him no fear, and he advanced to harm them. However, his eyes fell on the child Jesus, and he stopped, marvelling at the glorious beauty and majesty of his countenance. Deeply touched he protected the travellers instead of harming them and hosted them in his cave. This was the means divine providence used to help the Holy Family, in this instance, not with an angel but by means of a thief who was transformed into an angel. Dismas offered everything he had, and the divine infant allowed himself to be caressed by that criminal. Upon seeing the respect of the thief for their child, Mary Most Holy solemnly assured him that he would be rewarded for his action before his death. Dismas continued his life of crime, but he always conserved the memory of that promise, trusting that it would be fulfilled.[9]

The Meditations of Blessed Anne Catherine Emmerich: The Dolorous Passion of Our Lord Jesus Christ, chapter 40, The Crucifixion of the Thieves

The vision gives similar background information as St Anselm's meditation but with the following additions:

The thief placed on the left side was much older than the other, a regular miscreant who had corrupted the younger.

And concerning the penitent thief's first encounter with Jesus:

The poor leprous child who was instantly cleansed by being dipped in the water which had been used for washing the infant Jesus, was none other than Dismas, and the charity of his mother in receiving and granting hospitality to the Holy Family had been rewarded by the cure of her child; while this outward purification was an emblem of his inward purification which was afterwards accomplished in the soul of Dismas on Mount Calvary through that sacred blood which was shed on the cross for our redemption.[10]

What can be seen particularly in these apocryphal accounts of the thieves' crucifixion are a number of literary devices, which, no doubt, provided the material to exploit the canonical accounts in order to enrich sermons and Christian teaching. The thieves no longer become generic wrongdoers but are given names that are variable between the sources. And in each case the thieves are given a historical framework, a story that singles out characteristics which are polarised between roguish and very bad, merely wayward and evil, penitent and impenitent, saved and damned.

The apocryphal stories and meditations embellish the deeds, motives and characters of each thief to make it easier to position them at the opposite poles of good and evil. The external reality of each thief gives the writer, teacher and homilist the imaginative freedom to speculate and construct the alleged hidden nature and the natural orientation of each man. It is much easier to depict the soul of one man as utterly bad and irredeemable, to demonise him, and to depict the other man as merely sinful but ultimately good, without worrying too much about the middle ground where most of humanity dwells.

It is also much less complex to present a scenario that makes answering the difficult question of why, given the same set of conditions – that is, the presence of Jesus – one person can see something that leads to belief, while another cannot make that leap and sees nothing of the mystery breaking in and is damned, when most people flounder somewhere in between in the no man's land of belief and doubt, in the dappled shades of good and bad. However, that being said, as a literary device it does afford the opportunity to seek a way that leads to bridging the gap between one state and another.

The bridge between the two, which brings balance, is the life lived by Jesus, the life taught by Jesus and the death of Jesus. Jesus is nailed between the two realms of Adam. The impenitent thief – the old Adam, sinful and rejected from Eden – and the penitent thief – welcomed back through the gate of Paradise, Adam brought back and returned to his rightful place. This is indeed Good News, but in the reality that is our everyday lives, people are not literary devices, examples, exhibits or props easily categorised as damned and saved. The thieves were flesh and blood with childhoods, families and histories. Did St Luke embellish the dialogue between Jesus and the thieves so that the reader can draw from it the lesson that one was damned and one was saved? Or is there more to say?

[4] Pope Benedict XVI, Joseph Ratzinger, *Jesus of Nazareth: Holy Week* (Catholic Truth Society London, 2011), p.211.

[5] J. K. Elliot (ed), *The Apocryphal Jesus: Legends of the Early Church* (Oxford: Oxford University Press, 1996), pp.28-29.

[6] Ibid., p.70.

[7] J. K. Elliot, *The Apocryphal Jesus: Legends of the Early Years* (Oxford: Oxford University Press, 1996), pp.80-81.

[8] William Wake and Nathaniel Lardner, *The Apocryphal New Testament: The Gospel of Nicodemus* (London: Simpkin, Marshall, Hamilton, Kent & Co, 1970), pp.81-82.

[9] 'The Saint of the Day: St Dismas – March 25'. Available at http://www.traditioninaction.org/SOD/j238sd_Dismas_03_12.html (accessed 18th November 2016).)

[10] 'The Dolorous (Sorrowful) Passion of Our Lord Jesus Christ', from the Meditations of Anne Catherine Emmerich. Available at: www.jesus-passion.com/dolorous_passion_of_our_lord_jesus_christ_htm (accessed 14th November 2016).

Chapter 2
Contrasting pairs in Luke's Gospel

If the incident with the thieves is taken in isolation, it is just a short step to conclude that one was saved and one was damned. However, within the larger context of St Luke's Gospel, the reader comes to appreciate not only that, 'The doctrine proper to the Gospel of Luke is above all the gentleness and forgiveness that were the hallmarks of Christ's ministry',[11] and the constant emphasis on salvation (this will be discussed in more detail in chapter 3), but also that the pairing of the thieves and the relative positions that they each take throughout their dialogue are part of a number of pairings that appear in the text of St Luke that serve a similar purpose: the comparison of opinions in relation to the purpose and activity of God.

> 'Behold, I stand at the door and knock; if any one hears my voice and opens the door, I will come into him and eat with him, and he with me.'
> *Revelation 3:20*

Words taken from the Revelation of St John. Words written to the church of Laodicea. A community described as neither hot nor cold; a community that deserved to be called 'wretched, pitiable, poor, blind, and naked' (3:17). These words of St John inspired William Holman Hunt to paint the famous *The Light of the World*. The door at which Jesus is knocking is the door of the human heart, the life of every man, woman and child. The descending darkness indicates that Jesus has been standing and knocking for a good while; His feet are poised away from the door, indicating that the time of departure is drawing close and Jesus will leave and knock no more.

A closer inspection of the door itself shows that it has no handle. This door can only be opened from the inside because Jesus will only enter through the door of the human heart if it is opened voluntarily and He is invited in. As Hunt said, in its closed position it symbolises 'the obstinately shut mind'.[12] The door has been closed for a long time, for its hinges are rusty and the weed growth is so prolific that they hinder the door from opening just as the strangling, twining tendrils of sin prevent a life from being opened to the life-giving light of Jesus. Fruit lies discarded, rotten, decomposing, like so many responses to Jesus' invitation. In the darkness a bat can be seen flying about, a symbol of ignorance and ultimately a symbol of choice. The gift of freedom and choice is ours to make. Does the door remain closed or is it opened to the King of Glory? Do we choose the darkness of ignorance and self-delusion or the light of intimacy and salvation? St Luke, in the various pairings dotted in the body of the Gospel, poses the question time and again, and with the thieves this choice and the final reality of that choice is at its most explicit.

Former Archbishop Rowan Williams makes the point very clear. He writes:

Only three human individuals are mentioned in the creed; Jesus, Mary and Pontius Pilate: that is, Jesus; the one who says 'yes' to him; and the one who says 'no' to him. You could say that those three names map out the territory in which we all live. Through our lives we swing towards one pole or the other, towards a deeper 'yes' or towards a deeper 'no'. And in the middle of it all stands the one who makes sense of it all. Jesus – the one into whose life we must all try to grow, who can work with our 'yes' and can even overcome our 'no'.[13]

In the most extreme cases where a person's 'no' is bold, determined and immoveable, those who have made themselves utterly deaf to God's promptings, to quote Williams again, '[then] the most truthful image we can have of hell is of God eternally knocking on a closed door that we are struggling to hold shut'.[14]

St Luke presents these extreme positions in the personal attitudes of the thieves. There is the 'yes' of the penitent thief and the 'no' of the impenitent thief, and between them Jesus opens His arms of forgiveness and welcome to them both from the cross. But there are others in St Luke's work who swing between these opposite poles of 'yes' and 'no' by varying degrees before we reach the episode of the thieves. Can these other examples provide further insight into the thieves' response and what the reader might think their outcome will be? Some of these contrasting characters will manifest obvious dispositions of their positive or negative attitude towards openness to God, while others may be more subtle and reflect normal human behaviour given the existence of other formative circumstances.

Taken in the order they appear in St Luke's Gospel, we have the contrasting figures of Zechariah and Mary the mother of our Lord, Jesus and John the Baptiser, the Prodigal Son and his unforgiving brother, the rich man and Lazarus, the Pharisee and the tax collector, and finally the penitent and impenitent thieves.

Zechariah and Mary

Beginning with Zechariah and Mary as a deliberate contrasting pair isn't immediately obvious, at least not as obvious as some of the pairings that St Luke gives the reader. And yet, when the reader notices how both of these God-fearing, unremarkable people respond to a direct encounter with a messenger from God, it will be noticed that there is gravitation towards the positive and negative poles previously mentioned.

Zechariah is confronted by the archangel Gabriel in the Temple and is informed that his wife Elizabeth will provide a son despite her old age. Zechariah's response is telling. He replies, 'How shall I know this? For I am an old man, and my wife is advanced in years.' Gabriel replies, 'Behold, you will be silent and unable to speak until the day that these things come to pass, because you did not believe my words which will be fulfilled in their time' (Luke 1:18-20).

The question to Gabriel is a demand for proof, the request for a sign. His request is indeed granted, but not in the way that Zechariah expected or wanted. Being struck dumb is the result of Zechariah's lack of faith; it is also a sign of the genuineness of Gabriel's message.

Within the Syriac Poetic tradition, an anonymous dialogue poem between the Archangel Gabriel and Zechariah speculates on Zechariah's lukewarm response:

13. ANGEL: For what reason do you doubt and not give credence?
Why is it difficult for you to believe me?
In the Lord's hands it is possible
For something to be established out of nothing.

28. ZECHARIAH: The Lord knows He is hidden
And all thoughts are revealed before Him:
Even if I should accept your words with my lips,
My heart is still unwilling to listen you.

32. ZECHARIAH: Would that my intellect consented, sir,
And that my doubt were uprooted;
For it is quite clear to me that the Lord is able,
Yet I find it difficult to give credence to your word.

38. ANGEL: As long as you still do not believe what I have said
And my words do not appear true in your mind,
You shall be silent and dumb
Until these things have taken place indeed.[15]

Then there is the meeting of Gabriel with Mary. The message of Gabriel is equally as astonishing and miraculous, and as unlikely as Zechariah's, and the prophecy of Jesus' birth also elicits from Mary a question: 'How shall this be, since I have no husband?' (Luke 1:34). This is a far more positive question than Zechariah's. It is not a question that demands; it is a question that asks how this particular promise will come true owing to the particular circumstances that under ordinary conditions would mean that it would not be possible.

Turning again to another anonymous poem of the Syriac tradition, the author imagines a dialogue between Mary and Gabriel in the same way that the previous poet envisioned a dialogue between Gabriel and Zechariah, only in Mary's conversation there is a much more open, discerning attitude in comparison to Zechariah's unbelief. After a lengthy discourse, Mary is brought to the point of saying:

> **38. MARY**: In that case, O angel, I will not answer back:
> If the Holy Spirit shall come to me,
> I am His maidservant, and He has authority;
> Let it be to me, sir, in accordance with your word.[16]

Mary's response is not one of a lack of faith, but of a faith seeking to somehow comprehend the magnificent work of God, who chooses someone of such a lowly estate to be the bearer of Himself in the humanity of Jesus.

Immediately, the first contrasting pair displays a set of responses that differ when in the presence of the closeness of God. Zechariah feels the need for God to prove Himself further through Gabriel His messenger. His request for a further sign comes from a heart that has already determined what is required for God to be God, in contrast to Mary's heart that is at complete service to God and desires to make that service more perfect. The irony here, of course, is that being a priest of the Temple, Zechariah is the one whose profession sets him apart for the very purpose of God's service.

The thieves also find themselves in very close proximity to God, but how does that closeness make them react?

Jesus and John the Baptist

The second contrasting pair, like Mary and Zechariah, are not obvious candidates that demonstrate easily recognisable characteristics that are poles apart, but still (albeit in a very limited way with one of the pair), respond in a 'yes' and 'no' manner (the response by one of the pair isn't so much a 'no' but more of a 'don't know'). The pair in question is that of Jesus and John the Baptist.

To compare the two figures in order to create a line of argument about St Luke's use of pairings seems to be forcing the issue too far in the case of Jesus and John, for not only are their lives bound very closely together, but also their individual goals are set towards the same end. But there is one incident that may help to further understand the scene at Golgotha with the thieves, as a consequence of these two lives coming together.

The incident falls between several significant events in the ministry of Jesus. After healing the slave of the centurion and raising the dead son of the widow of Nain, but before receiving the sinful woman who anointed His feet with tears and oil, Jesus receives two of John's disciples who have been sent by John with a question: 'Are you he who is to come, or shall we look for another?' (Luke 7:19). Although Luke omits the detail of where John is at this point, we know from St Matthew's Gospel that he is in fact imprisoned (Matthew 11:2).

Like Zechariah, John poses a question. It is a question that seeks clarification, and contains elements of doubt and confusion. Was this Jesus the man that John so confidently proclaimed 'the Lamb of God' (John 1:29)? After all, John was expecting something different, someone who would exercise a fiery judgement (Matthew 3:7-12). His expectation of Jesus is not the same as the reality of Jesus.

So what is the reality? How does Jesus confront John's anxiety and doubt?

Jesus doesn't correct John through his disciples by argument or theological debate. He simply tells John to do the very thing that John has done. John pointed towards Jesus and told the people to 'look':

> Go and tell John what you have seen and heard: the blind receive their sight, the lame walk, lepers are cleansed, and the deaf hear, the dead are raised up, the poor have good news preached to them. And blessed is he who takes no offense at me.
> *Luke 7:22-23*

Jesus' actions and deeds are demonstrations of the fullness of the Kingdom breaking in, and all those who have ears to hear and eyes to see will come to realise that these signs make God's truth known and are invitations to believe. But these signs are not done in isolation; they are not to be detached from the person who makes them happen, the one who, in the words of Simeon, is THE sign who won't be obvious to all or accepted by all, and as a result, some will be lifted up but some will indeed fall (Luke 2:34-35).

For a moment there in prison, it isn't at all obvious to John whether Jesus is the one, the ultimate sign from God, or not. However, to fully appreciate this apparent wobble in John's faith, the context of his questioning must be taken into account. The darkness of a prison cell, the diminishing of hope, an extremely bleak present and future all aid in undermining any confidence that he once had in Jesus, and reflect a soul struggling to rise above the limitations placed upon him by his incarceration.

John's prison experience, this crisis in his life, is the context for his questioning and doubt. Any life crises will always determine and lay bare the stuff of which we are truly made. The effect of a situation like John's, where options are non-existent and choices are closed down, where one's existence becomes concentrated to a small point, will result in the stripping of the self to the most important things. For most people that usually means self-preservation at all costs. For John, his heart is still focused on Jesus, even if that focus is temporarily blurred, but where do the two thieves focus in their particular crisis?

The Prodigal Son and his brother

Next on the list of contrasting figures are the two brothers in the parable of the Prodigal Son (Luke 15:11-32). This story, told by Jesus, comes very close in structure and depth of meaning when compared with the verbal exchange between Jesus and the thieves in St Luke's narrative, and it is important in its interpretation of some of the inner dynamics of the people involved in the drama of the crucifixion. There are many levels of interpretation to the parable of the Prodigal Son, and when the story is described with reference to a devoted father who stands between his two equally loved sons, then a different kind of enquiry can be explored concerning the thieves.

The parable that Jesus taught about the errant son is one of three similarly meaning parables that draw the hearers to appreciate the joy of something that was once lost being found again – in the case of this particular story, a person, a younger son. But the story also includes another son, an elder brother who in many ways is also lost and cannot, or will not, see what is before his very eyes and so remains lost – or, to be more specific, the reader is left wondering because St Luke leaves the story in mid-air.

Between the two brothers and their differing personalities is the ever-present loving father. The father does not stand in the way of his younger son's decision to claim his inheritance and leave the family home to wander in far and unfamiliar lands. This sojourn is not just a physical separation from home; it is also a spiritual and moral distancing, an interior estrangement from the father and all those personal attachments and ties of identity that make him authentically himself. His decision for autonomy results in losing his very self.

Freedom without limit, without boundaries, without responsibility, renders this younger son a slave, at which point he realises where a true authentic existence lies, where the inner healing of reconciliation brings him back to himself as he turns his face towards the father. On his return, the father sees him and welcomes him with a passion that is symbolic of witnessing someone rising from the dead.

Now the elder son makes an entrance. His words and the emotions behind them betray an attitude that indicates a man who is also alienated from his father and his brother. He too is in a far country, racked with bitterness, contempt and self-pity. The language he uses reveals the heart that beats within. The tragedy revealed in the discourse between the older brother and the father is the brother's failure to recognise his own position as a much-loved son, and his blindness to the love that is extended to him in equal measure. Can the same be said of the thieves when the spotlight of the parable is shone into the darkness of that intimate group on Golgotha?

Lazarus and the rich man

It would seem that the most (erroneous) comparison to make with the pairing of Lazarus and the rich man (Luke 16:19-31) with the two thieves is one that defines a post-mortem fate. It would be an easy conclusion to come to; however, it isn't a conclusion that the crucifixion narrative supports – not in the case of the unrepentant thief, anyway. But what does stand out with this particular pairing is a theme that we have come up against previously: in the case of the rich man, a request for a sign.

Perishing in Hades, the rich man pleads that Abraham may send Lazarus back; firstly to ease his suffering, which in itself is a sign of selfishness and arrogance, for he thinks that even now when the tables have been turned, he can still order Lazarus around; and secondly to send Lazarus back to the land of the living to warn his brothers that this is the fate that awaits them if they do not change their ways. Abraham's answer is direct and to the point. To paraphrase, he tells the rich man that there have been plenty of evidence and opportunities to know the good things that wait for all those who recognise that God is a real and living presence, and if he indeed recognised one iota of this reality it would have spilled over into the care of those less fortunate. In the words of modern-day secular antagonists, 'What the rich man asks for is empirical evidence!'

Lazarus, on the other hand, epitomises the unfortunate 'non-person' so characteristic of St Luke's Gospel, a person bereft of anything or anyone that could mediate hope. But Lazarus' name hints at something else. In Hebrew, Lazarus means 'he whom God helps', and may be an indication that Lazarus, despite his material and physical poverty, made room for God in his life. His state as an outcast, poor and hungry, ignored and overlooked, would certainly have qualified him for being the recipient of God's help. Would it be true to say that the same help was available to both thieves at Golgotha?

The Pharisee and the tax collector

The final pair that stands out in St Luke's cast list is that of the Pharisee and the tax collector (Luke 18:9-14); one man who parades his virtues and the other who laments his vices.

The Pharisee congratulates himself on how wonderful he is, how self-assured he is. He is so absorbed with himself that his so-called communion with God is just a litany of self-worship. He fails to have any meaningful relationship with God because he blocks his own view; he stands in his own way of ever seeing God. The Pharisee's ego is so big he might as well have stopped his prayer after those opening words, 'I thank you that I am...', with all the theological implications of the designation 'I am'.

This is not a pleasant character to be around, for he will never be aware of the value of another human being, especially one as low and insignificant and despised as the tax collector: this creature, this parasite that his superior eyes have the immense displeasure to look upon.

The tax collector, on the other hand, has let go of any false image that he may have of himself. Difficult and painful as it obviously is for him, the act of self-scrutiny brings him to a place where he knows that without the help of God he would be unable to accept himself as he is and be given the strength and courage to move forward into a greater freedom.

In coming to a place where he recognises his true self, he is able to receive from God a love that is life changing. The Pharisee fosters a dangerous attitude that would no doubt, in time, have major implications for his fellow human beings, except, of course, those he could use to continue to inflate his ego. Being sufficient of oneself and standing in superiority over others gives licence to treat all others with complete indifference. The best that this attitude will ever do for those deemed inferior will be to ignore or belittle; the worst that this mindset might be capable of is to eradicate the inferior all together.

The attitude of the Pharisee throws the reader back to the very beginning of the book of Genesis and the original lie that festers by varying degrees in all people. At the heart of sin lies the human denial of our own creatureliness, and a refusal to accept dependency on God and on each other. If one wants to be like God in the sense of wanting to *be* God, self-contained and in need of nothing, then there is a danger that relationships are not needed either. But humanity is not like God in that sense. People can only be themselves, truly themselves, when in relationship and open to the One from whom sin cuts them off.

God's hand is forever outstretched in love and acceptance. As Pope Benedict XVI said, 'Only being loved is being saved, and only God's love can purify damaged human love.'[17] The tax collector indeed saw something of his sin, his detachment from God and his neighbour. But, more importantly, he grasped the hand of love that would guarantee his redemption.

The similarities in attitude that the tax collector and the Pharisee share with the two thieves are too obvious to ignore. Is St Luke using, in presenting a number of contrasting pairs before facing the final pair, a literary device to get the reader to see much more in the relationship of the thieves with the crucified Jesus than just a simple saved/damned outcome?

[11] *Congregation for Divine Worship and the Discipline of the Sacraments, Homiletic Directory* (London: Catholic Truth Society, 2014), p.7.

[12] W. H. Hunt, *Pre-Raphaelitism and the Pre-Raphaelite Brotherhood* (London: Macmillan, 1905), p.350-351.

[13] Rowan Williams, *Tokens of Trust* (Norwich: Canterbury Press, 2007), p.76.

[14] Ibid., p.151.

[15] Sebastian Brock, *Treasure House of Mysteries. Exploration of the Sacred Text Through the Poetry in the Syriac Tradition* (New York: St Vladimir's Seminary Press, 2012), pp.132-133.

[16] Ibid., p.141.

[17] Pope Benedict XVI, Joseph Ratzinger, *'In the Beginning...': A Catholic Understanding of the Story of Creation and the Fall* (London: T&T Clark, 1995), p.74.

Chapter 3
The thieves and the gentleness of Jesus

Commentators on the third Gospel seem to enjoy employing an alliteration of words in their endeavours to capture the essence of what St Luke understood to be the most important aspect of the life and ministry of Jesus. For example, John Pridmore uses the triple description of 'the last, the least and the lost'.[18] Patrick Whitworth uses the similar 'the loser, the lonely, and the lowly', alongside their opposite group 'the sleek, the successful and the slick'.[19] Another, which seems perfectly applicable to all that St Luke writes about, could be, 'the saviour, salvation and the saved'.

The language of salvation is certainly substantial in St Luke's Gospel, and is unparalleled when compared to the other Gospel writers:

Of the three Synoptic Gospels, only Luke speaks of Jesus as 'Saviour.' John gives him this title only once, when the Samaritans who have been moved by the witness of the Samaritan women declare that, 'this is truly the Saviour of the world' (John 4:42). Likewise, the word salvation which is so important for us and for the whole Church does not appear in Matthew or in Mark.[20]

The Greek words *soteria, soter* and *sozo* are words that appear many times in St Luke's Gospel and can be translated to include such meanings as 'deliverance from', 'salvation from', 'saviour' and 'to save'. For St Luke, the concern of Jesus to heal and bring salvation is so rooted in his Gospel account from beginning to end that it provides a key to unlock the Gospel as a whole. As much as the other roles of Jesus as Prophet, Priest and King are just as important, for St Luke, Jesus' primary role is that of Saviour. One writer, emphasising this role, condensed St Luke's work into one salvific sound bite:

> Salvation is expected in the birth narrative, heralded by John the Baptist, demonstrated in the Galilean ministry, presented in preaching and teaching, resisted by the religious authorities, accomplished in his death and resurrection, and continued in the post resurrection narrative of Acts.[21]

Through all these many and varied ways, St Luke presents to the reader the real possibility of salvation in situations that are both unexpected and seemingly hopeless, at least by human standards. And this is not a declaration of salvation at all costs, a trivialising of salvation, but a demonstration that in the gentle and merciful hands of the Saviour even the irredeemable and the meaningless are caught up in a world of all things being made possible.

The first indication that warns the reader to be prepared to have all limited assumptions and narrow thinking challenged are the words spoken to the Blessed Mary by the Archangel Gabriel, who greets Mary with the startling news that she is to conceive of the Holy Spirit and bring forth a son who is to be called Jesus, who will be the Son of the Most High God. And then Gabriel announces:

'And behold, your kinswoman Elizabeth in her old age has also conceived a son; and this is the sixth month with her who was called barren. For with God nothing will be impossible.'
Luke 1:36-37

Similar words to these are also on the lips of other messengers of God, the trinity of visitors who come to Sarah and Abraham at the oaks of Mamre in chapter 18 of Genesis. Abraham is told that, despite their advanced age and Sarah's inability to have children, she will indeed conceive. Sarah's response is well known: she laughs at the impossibility of such a suggestion. However, Abraham is challenged by the Lord because of her response:

The Lord said to Abraham, 'Why did Sarah laugh, and say, "Shall I indeed bear a child, now that I am old?" Is anything too hard for the Lord?'
Genesis 18:13-14

St Luke isn't finished with this aspect of the nature of God that makes the impossible possible, for it appears again in a slightly different context in chapter 18. Here the disciples are questioning the criteria for salvation in relation to the rich young man who lacked one thing: the ability to let go of his wealth. Picking up the conversation at verse 26, the disciples ask, 'Then who can be saved?'

But Jesus replies, 'What is impossible with men is possible with God' (Luke 18:26-27).

Once again the impossible becomes possible, and here it is in the context of salvation, underlining the reality and alerting the reader to the fact that with and in and through God the narrow categories of life that we so often work with, the natural inclination to reduce the working-out of God's purpose to humanity's own limited horizon and vision, limit all people to accept hopeless situations and be blind to what God can achieve.

There is a lesson here to be learned, and how life would be transformed if it were to be embraced! St Luke shows the reader that Jesus is the possibility of God incarnate. And if all people who strive in their discipleship of Jesus, or – to use a phrase of St Paul's – 'put on Christ', were to practise this attribute and fill all thoughts, words and deeds with this divine characteristic, then a Christian life would be a gateway and a signpost for all people to see that the impossible can happen when God's vision is allowed to act freely and with cooperation.

Salvation and redemption are at work when lives that are worn down and exhausted by the constant dead ends of impossibility are given hope which says that nothing is impossible when the grace and goodness and mercy of God are brought to bear in any given situation. Pastoral care; the love of neighbour; loving one's enemies; the healing of the four-fold relationship between ourselves and God, within ourselves, between ourselves and our neighbour, and between ourselves and the environment, are all achievable because we carry in ourselves, and are carried by, Christ who is the God of all that is possible.

The possibilities of God fill the landscape in which we have our existence, and the context through which we are able to do anything in His name. It is the foundation that enables trust in God to become an achievable goal, and the context in which an eternity in His company is a gift offered to all. God is the God of impossible made possible, of *Creatio ex nihilo*, creation out of nothing; a world where a virgin conceives, where God becomes man, where the dead are raised to new life, and where the invisible becomes visible. The flow of the impossible made possible allows the formless to have form, the uncontainable to become containable, a common criminal to be given the keys to Paradise, where the sign of the cross makes the cherub who bars the way to Paradise lower his flaming revolving sword. Even the Church Father Tertullian, when reflecting on the resurrection of Jesus, was moved to comment, '*Certum est quia imposibile*,' 'It is certain because it is impossible.'

To say that all things are possible with God is another way of describing and drawing upon the spaciousness of God, where people are given a large space in which to be and to become, while at the same time offering our neighbour the opportunity to be and to become. But sin has a tendency to reduce this spaciousness, to restrict God in the multiple opportunities to make the impossible part of the wider fabric of life for all people, to close down imagination and curtail creativity (even to hinder the miraculous, maybe). When sin abounds, focus on God is lost, and the result of this is not spaciousness but claustrophobia, and a blinkered narrow vision bereft of hope of experiencing the impossible. Nicholas of Cusa put it well when he said, 'God is an intelligible sphere, the centre of which is everywhere and the circumference nowhere.'[22]

The Blessed Virgin Mary provides a wonderful example. At the Annunciation, Mary's can be seen as a life that is utterly God centred and God focused, and it is this life that enables the impossible to become possible as a result of her selfless 'yes'. Mary's 'yes' is the key to the Incarnation. By her 'yes' she becomes the *Theotokos*, the God-bearer, and as a consequence Mary the Mother of God becomes a much-loved theme for iconographers. And it is no surprise that St Luke is accredited with being the first iconographer. There is one type of icon that is particularly pertinent to this discussion: that of Mother of God *Platytera*; *Platytera* being the Greek word for 'spacious', 'boundless', 'wider than', 'she whose womb is more spacious than the heavens'.

The created becomes the abode of the Creator, Who redeems not only the whole of humanity but the whole cosmos as well. 'For in this Rose contained was Heaven and earth in lytle space.'[23] The one who bears the child holds within her womb the whole of creation, and creation itself responds at the birth of Jesus.

An Orthodox liturgical text used during the celebration of Christmas rejoices with these words:

What shall we offer you Christ, who for our sake descended to earth as man? What creature of your creation thanks you? The angels offer you a hymn; the heavens a star; the wise men, gifts; the shepherds their wonder; the earth a grotto; the wilderness a crib; and we offer you a virgin mother.[24]

So much that seems impossible is made possible by a single 'yes', the total act of giving oneself over, abandoning oneself to the vision that God longs to put into action ever since the disobedience of Adam; the vision that is the working-out of His love. God's spaciousness is the playground for all things to be made possible. And when it is remembered that Mary is also an image of the church, the reality that with God all things are possible no longer becomes a piece of abstract theological thought but a mandate for the church to be the vehicle and the enactor and the symbol of all things being possible. When the church sets Christ before it, and its members join their 'yes' with Mary's, then the dividing walls of what seems impossible are brought down, and God has room to 'breathe'.

It was once said by an eminent churchman, 'nothing on earth is more transforming than a Church in love'.[25] A church in love is a community that occupies a large space and invites others into that space unselfishly and unreservedly. Rowan Williams writes:

Faith is *inhabiting a larger world*. One of the problems of perception in our world today is that it so often looks as though faith leads you into a *smaller* world and makes smaller human beings, whereas those of us who try to live with and in it would want to say, actually, it's an immeasurably larger world.[26]

The spaciousness of God is a theme that appears frequently. For example, in Gregory the Great's (d.604) second book of the *Dialogues* depicting the life of St

Benedict, he describes the occasion when St Benedict was in prayer:

> Long before the Night Office began, the man of God was standing at his window, where he watched and prayed while the rest were still asleep. In the dead of night he suddenly beheld a flood of light shining down from above more brilliant than the sun, and with it every trace of darkness cleared away ... According to his own description, the whole world was gathered up before his eyes in what appeared to be a single ray of light.
>
> All creation is bound to appear small to a soul that sees the Creator ... The light of holy contemplation enlarges and expands the mind in God until it stands above the world.[27]

C. S. Lewis in his wonderfully imaginative book, *The Great Divorce*, offers a creative story to describe God's spaciousness as one draws nearer to the Divine life. In his dream, as he gets off the bus that travels between the depressing, grey, shadowy town that is Hell for some, Purgatory for others, and the bus terminus which is heaven, Lewis describes the scene thus:

> I get out, the light and coolness that drenched me were like those of summer morning a minute or two before the sunrise. I had the sense of being in a larger space, perhaps even a larger sort of space, than I had ever known before: as if the sky were further off and the extent of the green plain wider than they could be on this little ball of earth.[28]

Further into the dream, there is a fascinating reversal of the appreciation of God's spaciousness and what fallen humanity *thinks* spaciousness is. While Lewis is being guided by his great friend George McDonald, what Lewis perceives as space, 'the big gulf, beyond the edge of the cliff,' proves to be just the opposite:

> My Teacher gave a curious smile. 'Look,' he said, and with the word he went down on his hands and knees … and presently [I] saw that he had plucked a blade of grass. Using its thin end as a pointer, he made me see, after I had looked very closely, a crack in the soil so small that I could not have identified it without this aid.
>
> 'I cannot be certain,' he said, 'that this is the crack ye came up through. But through a crack no bigger than that ye certainly came.'[29]

The aperture between a shadowy half-life that tends towards oblivion and a new life full of light that tends towards union with God and realised potential puts the reader in mind of the teaching of Jesus in the prophetic pronouncements of Luke 13:22ff, where the path of salvation is through the narrow door. In St Matthew's description, which concludes the Sermon on the Mount (Matthew 7:13-14), Jesus says, 'For the gate is narrow and the way is hard, that leads to life, and those who find it are few.'

A life that leads to God, a life that endeavours to live in close proximity to God, in openness to Him to be transformed by His vision, is a life that opens on to possibilities that are as limitless as the space God occupies. And again this is witnessed in Mary's encounter with the angel, and with Elizabeth's encounter. The impossibility of Elizabeth's pregnancy is made possible by her proximity to God. This is to live in heaven on Earth, to live in a bigger space.

In contrast, the rich young man of Luke 18 could not part with his treasure, could not step out of his self-made prison, and was attached to his wealth by the chains of greed and desire. He occupied a small world of reduced possibilities. This is to live in Hell on Earth. So St Luke shows the reader that the pilgrimage towards God is also a pilgrimage into a bigger and bigger space of possibility. The possible only becomes impossible when a life is spent closed, inward looking and self-occupied. And then the impossible is of that person's own doing, not God's. To go back to Mary, it is the difference between, "*Let it be* to me according to your word," and, "*Let it not* be to me according to your word."

The reader of St Luke's Gospel is not out of chapter 1 and already the importance of the salvific message he wishes to proclaim is uppermost. The Magnificat, the song of Mary, speaks of what God has done, is doing and will go on to do through Jesus. The proud, powerful and rich will find themselves scattered and brought down, and the lowly and hungry are lifted up. This is a recurring theme in St Luke's Gospel, sometimes referred to as the 'Great Reversal'.[30] These reversals, which turn the order of the world upside down, continue to broaden the theme of salvation. Salvation disrupts the order of the world, for it offers an alternative version that runs counter to the established cultural norm to which people conform and by which they are deceived. Mary's song resounds throughout St Luke's Gospel as an alternative story whose foundations are truth and wisdom and love. This narrative will always challenge an unquestioning conformity to a world where these values are treated as weak and unproductive.

However, in light of humanity's beginning and the goal to which God is leading, would it be more correct to say that God's ultimate purpose isn't so much to turn the world upside down but to return it the right way up? The Bible begins in a world which is harmonious, where God walks about His creation and man and woman are in relationship with all aspects of that creation; a vision of a world that is the right way up. But then there is discord and enmity, firstly between man and woman; then between man, woman and God; and finally between man, woman and creation. The world begins to turn on its head, and this flawed perspective results in brother killing brother by chapter 4 of Genesis, a totally corrupt world by chapter 6, and all-out war by chapter 14! Mary's song gives voice to the decisive moment that God has been actively pursuing since those days of disobedience, the moment of turning the world back on to its feet and not on its belly. And just as the world began, so it will end, in a city with a river flowing with the water of life, with trees bearing fruit and healing leaves (Revelation 22). Once again the world is the right way up, and everything is restored to its original state of peace and harmony.

St Luke gives the reader two other songs, two further canticles that continue the theme of salvation: the song of Zechariah and the song of Simeon. Zechariah pronounces the calling of his son, the ministry of John. God has raised up a mighty saviour who will bring liberation, and it is to be John's task to prepare the way for the coming salvation (Luke 1:67-80). Simeon is a patient and righteous man whose expectations are finally realised when he takes Jesus in his arms and declares, 'Lord, now lettest thy servant depart in peace, according to thy word; for mine eyes have seen thy salvation' (Luke 2:29-30).

This is what salvation is. It isn't just some clever philosophical, theological, abstract theory; it is a child. Jesus is not only the bringer of salvation; He *is* salvation. With Jesus, the human race moves from the 'How' of salvation to the 'Whom' of salvation. Simeon confronts us in simple terms with the fact that if you want to know what salvation looks like, if you want to know what the action of God looks like, then this is it, the baby in his arms.

No discussion of St Luke's understanding of salvation (even a cursory look such as this), would be sufficient without mentioning the Nazareth sermon of Luke 4. For biblical scholars this is seen as St Luke's masterstroke, and is the definitive framework for all that Jesus sets out to accomplish in His life, ministry, death and resurrection. Termed His 'manifesto', it is the programme that Jesus commits to undertake:

And he came to Nazareth, where he had been brought up; and he went to the synagogue, as his custom was, on the sabbath day. And he stood up to read; and there was given to him the book of the prophet Isaiah. He opened the book and found the place where it was written,
'The Spirit of the Lord is upon me,

because he has anointed me to preach good news to the
poor.
He has sent me to proclaim release to the captives
and recovering of sight to the blind,
to set at liberty those who are oppressed,
to proclaim the acceptable year of the Lord.'
Luke 4:16-19

Further reading of St Luke's Gospel presents the working-out of this manifesto. In fact, by the time of chapter 7, the reader witnesses Jesus' promised actions among the least, the last and the lost.

But there is one more point to make in regard to the primary task of this book, that of the two thieves, which is worth pointing out. It doesn't concern what Jesus says from the scroll of the prophet Isaiah; it is what He *doesn't* say. For the next line of the Isaiah text states, '... and the day of vengeance of our God' (Isaiah 61:2b). Can we deduce from the omission of this verse from Jesus' manifesto that His interaction with humanity will be the fulfilling of salvation, restoration, healing, forgiveness and acceptance, and not vengeance?

As this question hangs in the air, the next chapter will look again at the words of the thieves and the dialogue with Jesus within the framework of St Luke's pairings and within this overall context of salvation. Is there more to be made of their respective 'yes' and 'no', more that St Luke wants the reader to understand than just the typical response to these companions of Jesus?

[18] John Pridmore, *The Word is Very You: Feasts and Festivals* (Norwich: Canterbury Press, 2010), p.78.

[19] Patrick Whitworth, *Gospel for the Outsider. The Gospel in Luke and Acts* (Durham: Sacristy Press, 2014), p.VI.

[20] Justo L. Gonzalez, *The Story Luke Tells: Luke's Unique Witness to the Gospel* (Michigan: Wm B. Eerdmans, 2015), p.61.

[21] Source unknown.

[22] 'Nicholas of Cusa, Also Nicholas of Kues and Nicolaus Cusanus', Great Thoughts Treasury. Available at www.greatthoughtstreasury.com/author/nicholas-cusa-also-nicholas-kues-and-nicolaus-cusanus?page=4 (accessed 14th November 2016).

[23] Anonymous, c.1420.

[24] Solrunn Nes, *The Mystical Language of Icons* (Norwich: Canterbury Press), p.43.

[25] Source unknown.

[26] Rowan Williams, *What is Christianity*? (London: SPCK, 2015), p.22.

[27] , Julian Stead OSB, *Saint Benedict. A Rule for Beginners* (New York: New City Press, 1994), p.39.

[28] C. S. Lewis, *The Great Divorce* (London: HarperCollins Publishers, 1946), pp.19-20.

[29] Ibid., pp.137-138.

[30] Justo L. Gonzalez, *The Story Luke Tells*, pp.29-44.

Chapter 4
The thieves in relation to Luke's other character pairings

The basis of this investigation into St Luke's account of the crucifixion is that St Luke wanted his readers to see much more in the detailed description of the thieves that accompanied Jesus, which the other Gospel writers deemed unnecessary. So far this exploration has attempted to show the various ways in which St Luke has portrayed the thieves as contrasting characters in a line of other contrasting characters and within a framework of gentleness and salvation. This now enables a closer look at the conversation between Jesus and the thieves in light of St Luke's theological programme.

St Luke first introduces the two criminals in verse 32 of chapter 23, and the first words that he reports Jesus saying after the act of crucifixion has taken place are words of forgiveness: 'Father, forgive them; for they know not what they do' (verse 34). So immediately the reader is given an indication, completely in keeping with St Luke's portrait of the mission of Jesus, of how Jesus draws everybody into the orbit of God's forgiving love. Then the mocking of Jesus begins, first by the rulers (verse 35), and then by the soldiers (verse 36), and thirdly by the impenitent thief (verse 39). The mocking by the thief to Jesus' left marks the beginning of the exchanges between those crucified, and it is these exchanges that this chapter will consider in greater detail.

'Are you not the Christ? Save yourself and us!' The thief continues the mocking that has already rippled through the various gathered groups. He asks a question which indicates that he already knows something of this man, something either seen or heard, which indicates that He has the capability as God's anointed to stop what is happening and turn the situation around. The thief, in effect, is looking for some sign, some proof, and he demands a response. Zechariah's response to Gabriel amounted to a similar request, albeit not on the same scale. If faith, as the writer of the Epistle to the Hebrews puts it, 'is the assurance of things hoped for, the conviction of things not seen' (Hebrews 11:1), then Zechariah was uncertain in hope and certain that he needed some qualifying proof first. Similarly, John the Baptist, in a context of maltreatment, requested a sign or some kind of explanation from Jesus. He knew the capabilities of Jesus, but in his doubt, could he have been misreading the signs? Now in prison, he was questioning THE sign, Jesus Himself: 'Where is the fiery judgement? Why is my interpretation of the Kingdom different from yours?'

The sign theme appears again with the parable of the rich man and Lazarus. 'Send someone back from the dead to my brothers,' he says, 'that will convince them.' In reality, the rich man is told, no such sign will make a difference. If there is little or no faith to begin with, even someone returning from the dead would be explained away, or yet another sign would be asked for. Ultimately, nothing would change.

Zechariah, John the Baptist, the rich man and the thief, by varying degrees look for something in addition to what they think they know already. Their partial understanding puts them on a course that doesn't deny the existence of God and His activity, but challenges God's vocation and authority. 'How will I know?' 'Are you the one?' 'If someone from the dead goes to them?' 'Are you not the Christ?'

These voices echo the same sentiments as the one Jesus encountered in the wilderness, the voice of the Satan, the devil, the adversary (this will be looked at as part of a different question in chapter 7). Listen to what Benedict XVI says about the Satan's words in relation to Adam's temptation:

> Temptation does not begin with the denial of God and with a fall into outright atheism. The serpent does not deny God; it starts out rather with an apparently reasonable request for information, which in reality, however, contains an insinuation that provokes the human being and that lures him or her from trust to mistrust.[31]

And as Rowan Williams once said, 'Mistrust is always connected with the sense of not being in control.'[32] None of our questioning subjects is in control. They are no longer working to their own agendas, even if some of those agendas are not too far from the truth, as in the case of Zechariah and John the Baptist, or are the cause of not being able to see the truth that is right in front of them, as in the experience of the rich man and the impenitent thief.

How different is the response of the penitent thief:

'Do you not fear God, since you are under the same sentence of condemnation? And we indeed justly; for we are receiving the due reward of our deeds; but this man has done nothing wrong.'
Luke 23:40-41

Firstly, he raises the importance of the fear of God, which takes the reader of St Luke's Gospel right back to the words of the Blessed Virgin Mary in the Magnificat: 'And his mercy is on those who fear him from generation to generation' (Luke 1:50). The fear displayed by the impenitent thief is the fear of self-preservation which becomes, in circumstances such as the one he is experiencing, debilitating. This is a fear that looks only to itself and closes off the possibility that God can do the impossible. It is a fear that locks a person into narrow ways of thinking and closes down God's activity, for it only sees hope in what can be achieved without looking to God. Fear concerns itself with the fragility of the earthen vessel alone, but in that concern the treasure of God's image that lies within is overlooked. This expression of fear is far removed from the constant refrain that runs through Scripture of, 'Do not be afraid', and of that spoken about by the psalmist (Psalm 111:10) and the writer of Proverbs (Proverbs 9:10), where the fear of the Lord is the beginning of wisdom. This is a fear that gives God His rightful place and solicits from His creation due reverence and right worship in a relationship of love.

The penitent thief shows fear also, but this is fear of God, and this fear brings him divine mercy. Archbishop Fulton J. Sheen writes:

> The thief on the right, on the contrary, thought nothing of himself, but about others, namely the thief on the left and our Blessed Lord. His compassion went out to the thief on the left, because he was not turning to God in this last hour of his life and begging for forgiveness … It is interesting to enquire why the merciful Saviour not only forgave the penitent thief but even gave him the divine promise, 'This day you shall be with me in Paradise.' Why did not our Lord address the same words to the thief on the left? The answer is to be found in the Beatitude of Mercy: 'Blessed are the merciful: for they shall obtain mercy.' Because the thief on the right was merciful and compassionate he received mercy and compassion.[33]

This reflects the parable of the Pharisee and the Tax Collector, not only in respect of the recipient of mercy but also with regard to the attitude that underlies the respective personalities, attitudes that mirror the respective personalities of the thieves.

The Pharisee and the tax collector present a window through which the virtue of humility and its opposite, the sin of pride, can be viewed. The natural course of this behaviour is summed up by Jesus at the end of the parable: 'For every one who exalts himself will be humbled, but he who humbles himself will be exalted' (Luke 18:14). The impenitent thief has a high opinion of himself and displays a demanding, accusative attitude in reaction to the humiliation of the situation. His life has been built on death and it ends up with death. The penitent thief, however, lowers himself, becomes humble, and is taken up to be with the Lord – the future that is available to every humble heart. He built on the little of life that was left to him, and received eternal life as a result.

St Benedict of Nursia provides further commentary on the spiritual benefits of humility at the end of chapter 7 of the Rule. He writes:

Now therefore, after ascending all these steps of humility, the monk will quickly arrive at the perfect love of God which casts out fear (1 John 4:18).

And an important comment that speaks to the situation of the penitent thief:

Through this love, all that he once performed out of dread, he will now begin to observe without effort, as though naturally, from habit, *no longer out of fear of hell, but out of love for Christ*, good habit and delight in virtue.[34]

At the top of St Benedict's ladder of humility stands a person who has ascended by descending, which is a very good description of the effect of the penitent thief's humble heart. The similarities in personal attitude between the Pharisee/impenitent thief and the tax collector/penitent thief and the resulting relationship with God are incredibly close. In both sets of contrasting individuals it will be noted that their past lives neither render them redeemed nor in a state of sin, but how each eventually relates to God. In a resource entitled *The Parables of Mercy*, written especially for the Jubilee of Mercy, a reflection given on the Pharisee and the Tax Collector includes the statement:

> The Pharisee's attitude was arrogant; the publican's was humble. Despite his long prayer the Pharisee is not justified, while the tax collector's brief prayer is sufficient for him to go home justified … Acknowledging oneself as a sinner before God is the necessary condition for being justified; the arrogance of people who think they are sinless does not prevail in this situation.[35]

Compare this statement with the words that pass between the thieves and the underlying attitudes of the words spoken, and there exists a commentary applicable to both.

The Parable of the Prodigal Son, when used as a hermeneutical tool for St Luke's Golgotha drama, has the ability not only to provide those comparisons between the penitent thief and the prodigal and between the impenitent thief and the prodigal's brother, but also to present a fascinating parallel with the father of the sons and Jesus. As the father stands between his sons in the parable, Jesus stands between the thieves, and if the moral of the parable is transposed on to the relationships thrown together on that hill of death, then something happens that shakes the reader out of any preconceived ideas.

Probably the most definitive commentary on the Parable of the Prodigal Son is that written by the priest and author Henri J. M. Nouwen. For him, the following statement sums up the heart of the story:

The open-endedness of the story ... leaves me with much spiritual work to do ... This is not a story that separates the two brothers into the good and the evil one. The father only is good. He loves both sons. He runs out to meet both. He wants both to sit at his table and participate in his joy. The younger brother allows himself to be held in the forgiving embrace. The elder brother stands back, looks at his father's merciful gesture, and cannot yet step over his anger and let his father heal him as well.[36]

In the same way that the younger son of the parable takes stock of his life and realises in a moment of clarity that he is lost and there is only one possible solution to be found, even if it is in a somewhat diminished relationship than he had previously enjoyed, the penitent thief also takes stock and he too realises that he has been wandering in darkness, lost and rejected. But as late in life's day as it is for the penitent thief, his decision to seek forgiveness and to draw his partner in crime into making the same decision brings him home to the company of Jesus and the Father. The moment of heartfelt penitence is the moment that his sinfulness unravels; it is the moment that he is reconciled to himself as he sees the truth of himself and accepts it, and in accepting it, in sweeping his house clean, he replaces the void with establishing a relationship with Jesus. With Jesus' arms spread wide on the cross, the penitent thief accepts the invitation and urges the impenitent thief to share in this moment of loving mercy and forgiveness. It is in the words of the penitent thief that he fulfils the Law and the prophets. He begins, at last, to love God in Jesus with all his heart, and to love his neighbour, the impenitent thief, as he urges him to repent in an attitude of concerned love. The penitent thief acts out of a sense of real compassion, in that he sees and feels his neighbour's pain, that of the unrepentant thief, as real as his own.

> And he said, 'Jesus, remember me when you come into your kingdom.' And he said to him, 'Truly I say to you, today you will be with me in Paradise.'
> *Luke 23:42-43*

The penitent thief simply asks to be remembered. He probably thinks that is as much as he deserves, but his request also contains a statement of Christological importance. The penitent thief recognises Jesus' true identity: the Father's Kingdom is the Kingdom of Jesus, and the promise made by Jesus to open the gates of the Kingdom to the repentant thief is evidence that the man who suffers and dies on the cross, frail and humiliated, is God incarnate with the authority and power to forgive sins and welcome into the Paradisiacal home a common criminal.

The moment of the penitent thief's entry into Paradise is beautifully and creatively captured in another of the anonymous Syriac dialogue poems, entitled 'The Cherub and the Thief'. In the poem, the cherub stands at the gates of Paradise, having been placed there after the banishment of Adam and Eve, and is charged with the task of barring the way to all humanity. It is only after an interrogative exchange between the thief and the cherub that the thief produces the cross and the cherub grants him entry:

12 CHERUB: You are indeed a thief, just as you have said,
But you can't steal into this region of ours:
It is fenced in with the sword that guards it.
Turn back my man, you have lost your way.

13 THIEF: I was indeed a thief, but I have changed:
It was not to steal that I have come here.
Look, I have got with me the key to Eden,
To open it up and enter: I will not be prevented.

And then later in the poem the thief produces the cross of the Saviour:

41 THIEF: O agent for the King, don't be upset;
Your authority is repealed, for your Lord has willed it so.
It is His cross that I've brought to you as a sign:
Look and see if it is genuine, and don't be so angry.

42 CHERUB: This cross of the Son which you've brought to me
Is something I dare not look upon at all.
It is both genuine and awesome, no longer will you be debarred
From entering Eden, seeing that He has so willed it.[37]

The Prodigal Son has set his heart straight and turns towards his true home and the forgiveness of his father. The only renewed relationship he hopes for is to be taken back as one of the hired hands. However, the father's generosity exceeds all his hopes, as the son is embraced and has honours lavished upon him. The penitent thief experiences nothing less. He asks to be remembered, only remembered, but at the welcoming outstretched arms of Jesus he has the entirety of the Kingdom lavished upon him. The poem tells of the thief assuring the cherub that he did not come to steal the Kingdom but, as it is often said, steal it he did.

---

[31] Pope Benedict XVI, *'In the Beginning...'*, p.66.

[32] Rowan Williams, *Tokens of Trust*, p.4.

[33] Fulton J. Sheen, *The Cross and the Beatitudes* (Missouri: Liguori/Triumph, 2000), p.30.

[34] Timothy Fry OSB, *The Rule of St Benedict in English* (Minnesota: The Liturgical Press, 1980), p.38 (emphasis mine).

[35] Pontifical Council for the Promotion of the New Evangelization, *The Parables of Mercy* (Indiana: Our Sunday Visitor Publishing Division, 2015) pp.77-78.

[36] Henri Nouwen, *The Return of the Prodigal Son. A Story of Homecoming* (London: Darton Longman and Todd, 1994), p.78.

[37] Sebastian Brock, *Treasure House of Mysteries*, pp.220-229.

Chapter 5
The thieves and healing

'Lord, I am not worthy to receive you, but only say the word and I shall be healed.' These words are very familiar to all who regularly attend the Eucharist, and are often said prior to the giving and receiving of communion. They could also function as an explanation of what is happening in the exchange between the crucified Jesus and the penitent thief. The penitent thief, in his rebuke to the thief on Jesus' left, gives voice to the just nature of their punishment. They are indeed 'not worthy'. But the penitent thief looks at Jesus, and in acceptance of his unworthiness, asks simply to be remembered. And, as previously noted, Jesus goes beyond the act of just remembering and utters the words that result in this unworthy man receiving salvation, receiving healing. The penitent thief receives the broken body of Jesus with a humble and contrite heart, and despite the nearness of death, he is healed.

The Communion response may be taken from the request of the centurion when Jesus enters Capernaum (Luke 7:1-10), but they may very easily be the words of the penitent thief, for although few in number, they have something of a Eucharistic understanding about them. It is

74

also difficult not to notice an echo of Jesus' words at the Last Supper when He takes and breaks the bread with the words, 'This is my body which is given for you. Do this in remembrance of me' (Luke 22:19). To his disciples He says, 'Do this and in doing it remember me', while to the thief He says, 'In remembrance of you I will do this' (grant him Paradise). In the Eucharist and with the thief, Jesus becomes the primary sacrament of healing. However, for the purposes of this chapter, a broader question of Christian healing will be considered, and how, in the most gruesome and painful of circumstances, healing can be talked about at all.

Many in hospital chaplaincies, in parish ministry and in the medical profession, where there is sympathy and an understanding of the religious and spiritual dimension of care, will have the privilege of being with terminally ill people, people who, medically speaking, have reached the point where the process of dying is irreversible, and the prospect of an actual cure, of the rejuvenation of cells and bodily systems, is no longer possible. And yet, on many occasions, these same people will not only display but give voice to a sense of being healed.

To be healed is much more than being cured, although it can indeed contain within its definition a physical curing. To those who find understanding in conventional wisdom there is confusion between the terms 'healing' and 'curing', with the two words and their definitions often used interchangeably. To be healed is to be accepting of one's situation, to be in harmony and peace with oneself, with others and with God. To be healed is to be reconciled with one's past and with one's future, whether that is a future of increasing ill health, or a future that is held solidly in the Christian hope of being in the nearer presence of God after death.

Health is finding meaning in life in the midst of a balanced harmony between body, soul and spirit, and when that harmony is challenged by sickness and dying. The Christian approach to suffering is knowing that in the midst of a life that is diminished by pain, God's strength can be revealed, and in being revealed can be sustaining. Of course, none of this should deny the evidence of Jesus' ministry of healing, of the miraculous cures of body and mind, or dismiss the possibility of the miraculous or the hope of the miraculous in our own time and circumstances.

The distinction between healing and curing can be extrapolated from the words of the two thieves, and how those words are the verbal expressions of the emotions and desires that define their true characters in the urgency of their situations. Each of the thieves petitions Jesus, each makes a specific request in the hope that his awful predicament will be transformed. In this the two thieves are in agreement. In an intolerable situation they turn to Jesus, but this is where the similarities stop. A closer look at each man's request will reveal something of the cure/heal difference.

The first thief to speak, the impenitent thief, says, 'Are you not the Christ? Save yourself and us!' Apart from the immediate alleviation of his present situation and the preservation of the 'self', there is no indication that he sees beyond the boundaries of the finite. He wants what is good for him, and the urgency of the situation demands that this immediate want is met. The tone of the demand would suggest a life that is used to getting its own way at whatever cost to anyone else. And just suppose, to speculate for a moment, he is granted his request? All the indications are that he would return to his former life. Nothing of the deeper significance of what is going on will have penetrated the shell of selfishness other than the relief of being freed from a situation of pain and suffering.

The impenitent thief's desperate plea is to be 'saved', and the irony is that he spits this demand at the one, the only one, who can truly save, truly redeem; but not just the body, which the impenitent thief desires the most, but his immortal soul as well. This man misses the opportunity and the invitation of being called out of his prison of selfishness, of his perpetual wandering in the dark, of satisfying his own needs, and accepting the moment where he can gaze on the figure of the Christ and realise that underneath the layers of his sinful actions, he too is made in the image of God, an image so long neglected and buried.

For the impenitent thief, then, to be saved is to return to a life of the flesh. And as St Paul teaches, a life lived according to the flesh is a life that is subject to 'fornication, impurity, licentiousness, idolatry, sorcery, enmity, strife, jealousy, anger, selfishness, dissension, party spirit, envy, drunkenness, carousing and the like' (Galatians 5:19-21). The alternative life has been nailed to a cross next to him, the death of the one who brings forgiveness, relationship with God and healing. To quote the words from the Church of England's Report, *A Time to Heal*:

> The real evidence of healing is a change in the
> individual as a result of knowing the risen Christ's
> saving and healing grace within them.[38]

St Luke evidences this change in attitude in response to the healing grace of Jesus during His earthly ministry in the incident of the ten lepers (Luke 17:17-19). The incident is fascinating in that there is a distinction made between being cured – in the case of the lepers the cure is being cleansed – and the fuller personal experience of being healed. Ten lepers plead for Jesus to have mercy on them, and He instructs them to go to the priests. As they go on their way, they are each cleansed, each one is cured, but only one of the lepers, when he sees he is cured, returns to give thanks and praise for his healing. The physical cure of the other nine does not result in the discovery of a deeper response that extends beyond the 'self'. The nine lepers may have been cured, but only one was healed, as demonstrated in the 'self-abandoning' in thanks to Jesus. This healed leper breaks through the claustrophobia of narrow, selfish thinking and recognises in Jesus not just another wonder worker who has satisfied a particular need, but an action of God that met the greatest need of all: the conversion of heart in thankfulness that the love of God in Jesus was just as much a gift for him, an untouchable person, impure through disease and nationality, outside the Covenant of Israel, as it was for God's elect.

Knowing that God loves unconditionally, whoever that person may be, wherever that person may be from and whatever stories culture may want to tell in order to exclude, is a wonderfully healing thing. But it cannot just stop with that reality. Recognising that God rejoices in every one of His creatures is just the beginning of an ongoing revealing of God's bigger vision, a vision that is transforming. The clearest picture of what God's vision looks like in all its fullness is there in the person of Jesus, and in order to become bearers of and transparent to that vision, humanity needs to grow towards and become like Jesus. If Jesus is the truly authentic human being, then humanity can only claim to be human 'becomings', for most of us are way down that scale of being like Jesus.

The few words uttered by the penitent thief on the cross present a person in the process of 'becoming'. His rebuke to the thief on Jesus' left is a statement that reveals his own emerging understanding, his own tentative steps towards the realisation that begins his movement towards healing. His question about the fear of God is an indication that he knows what the true fear of God means. Proverbs 1:7 comes to mind: 'The fear of the Lord is the beginning of knowledge; fools despise wisdom and instruction.' The fear of God is an attribute that the penitent thief is learning very quickly and which the impenitent thief seems incapable of grasping. However, fear of God is just the beginning, for knowledge of God must have as its goal the love of God, which the penitent thief is discovering even at this late time. Knowledge by itself is insufficient, for, as it is often said, even the devil and his minions have knowledge of God. The difference in practical terms between knowledge by itself, cold facts, and enlightening rhetoric which is transformed into love, is best summed up in a piece of advice given to ordinands by Bishop Michael Ramsey. He said, 'May it one day be said of you, not necessarily that you talked about God cleverly, but that you made God real to people.'[39]

Commending the faith, presenting the healing ministry of Jesus, is not only about delivering clear and precise theological and doctrinal arguments, as important as they may be. Neither is it about personal opinion devoid of a rigorous experiential and well-reasoned underpinning, but it is showing that all these disciplines combined make a difference and make the Kingdom of God visible. This is what the repentant thief begins to understand in his last moments. The words that Jesus addresses to him from the cross are not clever theological arguments of atonement theory, or wishful opinions. In St Luke's Gospel, the cross is a real demonstration of forgiveness, an action that penetrates the armour of self-delusion and a demonstration that the love that flows out in the blood and suffering of Jesus is the prescription for eternal life and salvation.

The repentant thief realises that he has spent a lifetime captive to his sinful nature and is brought to make confession, to admit his guilt. What he once thought of as a life lived in freedom, according to his own will and desires, has been the exact opposite. He has in truth lived like the impenitent thief, a life concerned with the finite, in the land of the shadow of death. However, in his proximity to Jesus and the dawning reality of the true nature of the One with whom he enters into meaningful dialogue, he begins to step into the life of the infinite, the light-filled uplands of eternity. Here is where true healing can be found.

To use one of the three principal categories of the healing ministry on which the Church of England document *A Time to Heal* is based, the penitent thief's words are 'prophetic'. He puts before his audience what is the bedrock of healing, and that is a consideration of the relationship between God, each other and the world, which results in the conditions to make a new start.[40] He makes a plea of forgiveness for all his misdeeds and those who have been implicated in those deeds. It is an attempt to put things right with the world that he has marred with his wrongdoing. He attempts to draw into the moment of confession and salvation his co-criminal. This shows an awareness of the 'other'. And finally he repairs his relationship with God and seeks union with Him in Jesus through his request to be remembered.

To return to the theological headings of the Church of England report, the penitent thief fulfils the 'prophetic' understanding of healing. He also goes on to fulfil both the 'visionary'[41] and the 'dynamic'[42] understandings. 'Visionary' because his actions beckon the reader towards a future and a glimpse of the Kingdom, the hope of creation renewed in perfect health and wholeness. 'Dynamic ... because Jesus is with us to the end of time: when we pray for his help, he comforts, strengthens and heals us, responding to our deepest needs': words again quoted from the report.[43]

The few words that pass between the penitent thief and Jesus sum up in microcosm the entire nature of Christian healing. When we reflect prayerfully on the words and the emerging change that results in the course of the conversation, then life is opened to God's healing. 'Remember me when you come into your kingdom':

> This is the cry of every humble human heart. It echoes our most fundamental human need: 'Jesus, remember me. Let me know that I matter; give me a chance to begin a new life; help me to find that total well-being we call salvation.'[44]

Intimacy with the author of life is to understand what true healing is. The penitent thief reflects this intimacy in his use of the name 'Jesus' in his request to be remembered. There is only one other place in St Luke's Gospel where this intimate use of the name 'Jesus' is found on the lips of a person longing for Jesus to do something, and that is the blind beggar at Jericho (Luke 18:35-43). At the plea of the blind beggar, Jesus heals him from his blindness with the words, 'Receive your sight.' Both the penitent thief and the blind beggar call upon the name of Jesus, and both 'see'. The blind beggar is healed of his physical blindness in response to having spiritual sight into the true nature of Jesus, while the penitent thief receives healing from spiritual blindness even though he can physically see.

The penitent thief opens himself up to Jesus and no longer hides behind falsehoods and lies. By laying bare his utter wretchedness, he places himself before the mercy and compassion of Jesus, and in return Jesus is able to confer on him a greater gift that goes beyond mere remembrance. This gift transcends the narrow definitions of curing or respite from life's inevitable demise and walk to the grave. For life offered in the nearer presence of God is healing that does not give the struggles of life the last laugh. The contrast with the impenitent thief, who physically and mentally is in the same predicament as his crucified partner, gives substance to what healing truly means when it is placed in the framework of knowing and handing over one's life to Jesus.

The activity of God in His creation is not always easily discernible or observable, but what makes it so in the relationship between the penitent thief and Jesus is the openness on the part of the thief to the proximity of Jesus. At this particular moment in time, this damaged and hurting life pushes open the door to God's activity through the sincerity of his prayer, his honesty about himself and his request to be immersed more in the divine life. Can it be said that this loving abandonment into the life of God somehow allows God more freedom to work? Rowan Williams thinks so:

> God ... always has the freedom to keep the door open and let new things emerge. But we can put ourselves more at the service of this freedom or less; we can give ourselves to it or resist it. And if we hold on to a picture of this kind, it may help a bit in thinking through this question of why some prayers are 'answered' and others are not. It can't be because God likes some people more than others or because some people know the right strings to pull or buttons to press ... All we know is that our prayer or our offering of some act of love or devotion can be one of the innumerable factors in a situation that may shift the balance of events and open the door further.[45]

The penitent thief does that very thing. He pushes the door open, and love and light and life come flooding through; healing enters and is offered a home. The impenitent thief, however, seems to keep the door firmly closed. In every other way there is no distinction between these two thieves. They both share an intimate proximity to Jesus, they both suffer and are punished for the same faults, in their own way they both call to Jesus, and Jesus loves them both equally. Neither one is better than the other. Neither deserves to be heard, neither has the advantage to manipulate the event, except that one comes humbly before God and re-establishes creatureliness towards the Creator and hears the word of salvation, while the other maintains his defiance and lives his last moments in rebellion. Only silence exists between the impenitent thief and Jesus, and bears a similarity with the situation Jesus faced in His home town of Nazareth. In Mark 6:1-6 there is a very revealing incident where Jesus admits that He is incapable of performing any miracles where people's hearts are so hardened. Love is offered, the hand of healing and salvation is offered, but it is rejected, and God will not act by force.

Bishop Morris Maddocks, one-time advisor to the Archbishop of Canterbury, was on record as saying that, for him, 'Christian healing is Jesus Christ meeting you at the point of your need.'[46] Using this inspired definition, it seems that the penitent thief indeed correctly perceives his needs and, in bringing them before Jesus, finds in Him the true offer of healing. The impenitent thief, on the other hand, doesn't know what he needs; he knows what he *wants* – he makes that clear enough – but while each person may have a clear idea of what is *wanted*, few may actually know what is *needed*. For the penitent thief it seems perfectly reasonable to interpret his words as a sincere prayer for Jesus to meet him at the point of his greatest need, a need to be forgiven, to be received, to be with Jesus for all eternity, to be healed. However, the impenitent thief seems to have little understanding of his needs, but much to say about what he wants. He wants to be released, he wants Jesus to demonstrate a kingship more in keeping with the world he is used to, a world of death and combat and overthrow of the powers that are responsible for the situation they are in. And to what end? Probably so that he can go back to his former life lived in separation from God and his fellow human beings. At its core, the prayer of the penitent thief is the prayer of Jesus himself: 'Thy will be done,' while the impenitent thief prays the prayer of every person turned in themselves: 'My will be done.'

There is a prayer written by an unknown Flemish author who was a contemporary of Thomas à Kempis, and part of it has this piece of advice:

Is there anything you need? If you like you can write out a long list of all your pride, all your touchiness, self-centredness, meanness, and laziness. Do not be ashamed; there are many Saints in Heaven who had the same faults as you; then prayed to me and little by little their faults were corrected. Do not hesitate to ask me for blessings for the body and the mind; for health, skill, success. I can give you everything and I always do give everything that is needed to make you holier.

'Everything that is needed to make you holier.' That is the crucial point. The two thieves in their respective requests seem to project one of them back down an already well-trodden path, while the other is set on a journey into holiness. The penitent thief's greatest need is union with Jesus, and that need is met; the impenitent thief wants to resume a life under his terms, which are unlikely to result in a growth in holiness, and he is met with silence.

The remarkable lesson here is that holiness is bestowed and eternity assured to a man with no chance of escaping the immense suffering being experienced. It is a sobering thought that Jesus was descended from a people who are beloved and chosen by God, but before they were a chosen people, they were one man, Jacob, who was given the name Israel while wrestling with God at the river Jabbok (Genesis 32:22-32). In the confrontation, his thigh was put out of joint and he was given a blessing. The people worthy to be called chosen from all other people and races are the people who *limp*, and it is from these people that God calls His Son. This is what healing looks like; this is where healing is to be found: in the blessedness of one who limps and in the pain of the crucified that is mindful of the presence of the Saviour and the hope of the world to come.

---

[38] The Archbishops' Council, *A Time to Heal: A Contribution Towards the Ministry Of Healing* (London: Church House Publishing, 2000), chapter 11, p.208.

[39] Michael Ramsey, *The Christian Priest Today* (London: SPCK, 1972), p.78.

[40] The Archbishops' Council *A Time to Heal,* p.262.

[41] Ibid., p.260.

[42] Ibid., p.267.

[43] Ibid., p.267.

[44] Stephen C. Rowan, *Words from the Cross* (Connecticut: Twenty-third Publications, 1989), p.23.
[45] Rowan Williams, *Tokens of Trust*, p.46.
[46] Morris Maddocks, *Twenty Questions about Healing* (SPCK, 1988), p.1.

Chapter 6
Good to the right, bad to the left

'And when they came to the place which is called The Skull, there they crucified him, and the criminals, one on the right and one on the left' (Luke 23:33). The four Gospel writers designate the position of the criminals crucified with Jesus as being on His right and on His left, but only St Luke makes the observation that the thief on the left is the bad thief, while the space occupied on Jesus' right is taken up by the good thief. Is there anything to be made from this right/left, good/bad symbolism?

This separation of the thieves to the right and to the left, with Jesus 'enthroned' on the cross between them, gives dramatic substance to the final judgement passage of St Matthew's Gospel (Matthew 25:31-46). The final judgement will be characterised by the separation of the sheep from the goats, the righteous from the cursed. Each group is given its designation depending on how they received Christ in the various needs of their neighbours. Those who met the needs of their neighbours and eased their burdens were doing the same to Christ. For this group of people, the Kingdom is prepared and entry is guaranteed. However, those who ignored the needs of their neighbours and walked on by are charged with treating Christ in the same manner. For this group, eternal damnation awaits. And while the verbal evidence seems to give weight to the association of the left being bad while the right is good, there is also a body of iconographical evidence that makes the same distinction.

One of the major iconographical representations of Christ is that of *Pantocrator*, Christ the Almighty, Christ the Lord of the Universe, the judge of the living and the dead. And probably the most famous of them all is that of the sixth-century icon, *Christ the Pantocrator*, from St Catherine's Monastery, Sinai (Plate 1). In this icon the face of Christ dominates, and the observer cannot help but notice the imbalance in the right and left of Christ's face. About this imbalance, Jonathan Pageau writes, 'The explanation most often given is that Christ's right represents his merciful side while his left represents his rigorous side.'[47] There is no doubt that the right side of Christ's face shows a kinder expression, while His left side, with His eye more piercing and the slightly pinched lips, gives a more severe look.

In icons that include the thieves, it seems that their positioning is theologically motivated to endorse what St Matthew says about the final judgement. However, there are some icons and pictorial representations of the crucifixion that leave the observer in no doubt. Take for example the fourteenth-century crucifixion altar frontal by Jacopo di Cione (Plate 4, page 113). It can be clearly seen that above the penitent thief are two angels carrying the man's soul off to Paradise, while above the impenitent thief are frighteningly dark depictions of devils preparing to carry his soul off to eternal damnation.

Plate 1 *Christ the Pantocrator*, sixth century, Mount Sinai, Saint Catherine's Monastery

Other artistic/iconographical techniques also work on the senses of the observer to underline the left/right, good/bad symbolism. Again it will be noted that in canonical iconography the body of Jesus tends to be turned towards the penitent thief, and their faces tend to be looking at each other. This in turn results in the body and face of Jesus being turned away from the impenitent thief. Occasionally the head of the impenitent thief will also be depicted as turning away from the figure of the crucified Jesus, highlighting his rejection of the saviour of the world. Along with the angels bearing up the soul of the penitent thief, some iconographers will also add a halo to the head of the thief. The presence of the halo is an indication that he is at last living in an intimate relationship with God, and is being bathed in His divine light.

Moving away from the figures and on to the cross of Jesus, there are some depictions of the cross, such as that of the Russian Orthodox Church (the *Suppedaneum* cross), which are shown with three cross bars: the top bar, known as the *Titulus*, containing the inscription written by Pontius Pilate, the longer crossbar (the *Patibulum*), and a slanted bar on which the feet of Jesus are nailed (Plate 2). The slanted foot rest rises at Jesus' right foot and points downwards at his left foot, again introducing a theological definition to the right/left symbolism. To quote again from Jonathan Pageau's article, the reason for the slanted foot rest is explained in a Russian iconography handbook:

Question: Why is the footboard of the Cross of Christ pointed with the right side up, and the left down, and the head of Christ is also inclined to the right? Answer: Christ makes His right foot light and lifts it above the footboard in order to lighten the sins of the ones who believe in Him. And His left foot he lowers on the footboard in order that those who do not believe in Him

Plate 2 Russian Orthodox Suppedaneam Cross

should be weighed down and descended into hell. His head is inclined to the right, that He might incline all the heathen to believe and worship Him.[48]

Plate 3 *The Crucifixion*, c.a. 1500, The Holy Trinity Cathedral of the Paulo-Obnorsk Monastery, Moscow Tretyakov Gallery

The right/left, good/bad motif, occasionally shows up in icons of the crucifixion, which seem, at first appearance, to be unrelated to the thieves. The icon entitled *The Crucifixion* from the Holy Trinity Cathedral of the Paulo-Obnorsk

Monastery shows an angel under Jesus' right arm introducing an allegorical figure representing the New Testament, while underneath his left arm another angel is driving away an allegorical figure of the Old Testament (Plate 3). There does seem to be in this symbolism a nod in the direction of supersessionism, of the replacing of Israel with the church. However, when this particular motif is extended to the thieves, their words and what their words reveal about themselves, it doesn't endorse a supersessionist theology but confirms St Luke's position on fulfilment.

The thieves and the Exodus

St Luke begins his Gospel by reassuring Theophilus that he can have confidence in this account of the events of Jesus' life, alongside other eyewitness accounts that have also been written about 'the things which have been accomplished among us' (Luke 1:1). St Luke therefore is concerned from the outset to show that what God has promised from the very beginning is finally reaching its goal, reaching its completion. If the thieves are approached as 'types' of the founding stories of the chosen people, then this theme of fulfilment comes clearly into view – to be specific, the Exodus from Egypt, and the Exile and return from captivity in Babylon.

If the death of Jesus is the moment when God acts to deliver all people from the bondage of sin and death once and for all, then the story of the liberation of God's people from Egyptian oppression in the event known as the Exodus will have a similar pattern and offer several parallels. The first parallel is between Jesus and Moses. As the risen Jesus walks with the two disciples on the Emmaus road (Luke 24:13-35), He demonstrates through the retelling of Scripture that everything experienced by them that day is already to be understood through the prophets, and, read correctly, the prophets' words have now been fulfilled. As Jesus explains, He begins with Moses (v 27). Jesus is a 'type' like Moses (see, for example, Matthew 2), and while it is beyond the scope of this book to draw out from St Luke's writings the many parallels, the words on the lips of St Peter in St Luke's second volume, The Acts of the Apostles, provide the link with the thieves and the Exodus theme. In the Acts of the Apostles, Peter, while urging repentance to the people gathered around him, says this:

> Moses said, 'The Lord God will raise up for you a prophet from your brethren as he raised me up. You shall listen to him in whatever he tells you. And it shall be that every soul that does not listen to that prophet shall be destroyed from the people.' [cf. Deuteronomy 18:15, 19.]
> *Acts 3:22-23*

So if Jesus is a 'type' of Moses, what did Moses do? In the story of the Exodus, Moses is raised up from among the people and becomes the bridge between the people and God, as God acts to liberate the people whom He has chosen from the bondage of slavery under Pharaoh and the Egyptians. When they were slaves, God heard their cry and, through the leadership of Moses, He leads them out (the Exodus) to the Promised Land, to a place where God would be in their presence. (For the full story read the Pentateuch, the first five books of the Old Testament, particularly the book Exodus itself.) In the story, the freedom of God's people begins under the cover of darkness, with the slaughter of an unblemished lamb whose blood would protect each household from the destroying angel who would pass over the dwelling, and the preparation of unleavened bread with herbs.

With these bare facts, the similarities with St Luke's crucifixion account can now be made. Jesus, like Moses, not only bridges the gap between God and man, He closes the gap completely and becomes the human face of God turned towards humankind. As the Passover sacrifice, the breaking of His body and the shedding of His blood becomes the means by which God delivers humanity out of the slavery and bondage of sin. The unrepentant thief is the image of the pre-Exodus people, a slave in the land of forces that cripple and bind and dehumanise. Marcus Borg, reflecting on the story of the Exodus, makes a comment that strikes a descriptive chord that applies well to this hypothesis:

As a story about God and us, what is it [the Exodus] saying? Our problem, according to this story, is that we live in Egypt, the land of bondage. We are slaves of an alien lord, the lord of Egypt, Pharaoh. It provocatively images the human condition as bondage ... It invites us to ask, 'To what am I in bondage, and to what are we in bondage?' ... The Pharaoh who holds us in bondage is inside of us as well as outside of us. Who is the Pharaoh within me who has me enslaved and will not let me go? What instruments of fear and oppression does he use, this Pharaoh who tries everything to remain in control? What plagues must strike him?[49]

The unrepentant thief is a slave to his passions. His 'alien' lord remains hard of heart and refuses to let him go, and he demonstrates an attitude that would suggest that the 'plagues' of condemnation, crucifixion and an unrepentant death will not release him from the firm grip of his imprisoning Pharaoh. Unlike the repentant thief, who confronts his 'plagues' and responds in the same way that Pharaoh eventually responds to Moses in the book of Exodus:

> Then Pharaoh called Moses and Aaron in haste, and said, 'I have sinned against the Lord your God, and against you. Now therefore, forgive my sin, I pray you, only this once, and entreat the Lord your God only to remove this death from me.'
> *Exodus 10:16-18*

It isn't a plea that Pharaoh sticks to, but the repentant thief does. His act of contrition comes from the heart, no longer a hardened heart, but a heart touched by the mercy of God through Jesus, who indeed leads him out of bondage to his 'Pharaoh' and takes him to the Promised Land: 'Truly, I say to you, today you will be with me in Paradise.' With a little religious imagination, the role of the thieves brings to mind the Exodus story, for not only do both reflect the true nature of God towards His people who cry out from their sufferings, but they also show the pre- and post-state of lives once bound but then freed.

One final point: the defeat of Pharaoh and the liberation of God's chosen happens under cover of darkness, 'at midnight' (Exodus 12:29), while at the moment the repentant thief distances himself from the unrepentant thief and casts off his bondage to sin, thus preparing the way for Jesus' promise of Paradise, 'there was darkness over all the land' (Luke 23:44).

The thieves and the Exile

In much the same way as the Exodus, the Exile is another of the most important experiences of the Jewish people that helped to define their theology and their relationship with themselves and God. During the reign of Zedekiah, the southern kingdom of Judah is besieged by king Nebuchadnezzar of Babylon. Jerusalem and the Temple are reduced to ruins, and the people of Israel are carried off into exile. The reason for this? The prophet Ezekiel writes:

> Thus says the Lord God to the land of Israel: An end! The end has come upon the four corners of the land. Now the end is upon you, and I will let loose my anger upon you, and will judge you according to your ways; and I will punish you for all your abominations. And my eye will not spare you, nor will I have pity; but I will punish you for your ways, while your abominations are in your midst.
> *Ezekiel 7:2-4*

It seems that despite the Covenant made between God's people and God, the Israelites are forever chasing after other gods and worshipping idols. God promised His people life; they in turn repay that promise with idolatry.

But it isn't the end for God's people, and just as the prophets are warning about the consequences of turning their backs on God, they also look forward to a renewed hope, a new covenant:

> I will be their God and they shall be my people ... for I will forgive their iniquity, and I will remember their sin no more.
>
> *Jeremiah 31:33-34*

From a life separated from God, there will eventually be a homecoming, and God will indeed be with His people once again, but in a new and quite remarkable way.

The unrepentant thief is an image of the pre-Exile people. He has spent a lifetime worshipping the idols of self-gain, self-fulfilment and, no doubt, personal pleasure, and his whole demeanour at Golgotha is one of self-preservation. He seems to have had his back turned to God for so long that he continues in that vein even though God in Jesus is within touching distance. It seems that he has been separated from God for so long that he no longer sees the possibility of a homecoming, unlike the repentant thief. He has a new heart, no longer a heart of stone. He sees before him the fulfilment of God's promise and he longs to be back home. The repentant thief is no longer in exile, no longer weeping by the waters of Babylon (Psalm 137); he is instead hearing words of peace as those who have turned to Him in their hearts (Psalm 85). The repentant thief had sown in tears; he went out weeping. He is now reaping and has returned home with shouts of joy (Psalm 126).

In a previous chapter, the story of the Prodigal Son was cited as a comparison example with the two thieves, and at this juncture another similarity can be made. It is important to remember that the parable told by Jesus about the brothers and the caring father is unique to St Luke's Gospel, and in respect to this N. T. Wright makes this observation:

> Years of scholarship have produced many commentaries on Luke and many books on the parables. But none that I have been able to consult has noted the feature which seems to me to be most striking and obvious. Consider, here is a son who goes off in disgrace into a far country and then comes back, only to find the welcome challenged by another son who has stayed put. The overtones are so strong that we surely cannot ignore them. This is the story of Israel in particular of Exile and restoration ... But Israel would return, humbled and redeemed, sins would be forgiven, the covenant renewed, the Temple rebuilt and the dead raised. What her god had done for her in the Exodus – always the crucial backdrop for Jewish expectation – he would at last do again even more gloriously. YHWH would finally become king, and would do for Israel in covenant love, what the prophets had foretold.[50]

Wright sees in the parable of the Prodigal Son a strong echo of both Exodus and Exile. So considering that St Luke's extended report of the thieves is unique to his Gospel, just like the parable, and there are parallels, then by association, loading the account of the thieves with an Exile/Exodus interpretation doesn't seem to be beyond the realms of possibility.

[47] Jonathan Pageau, 'Mercy on the Right. Rigor on the Left', *Orthodox Art Journal*, 15th January 2013. Available at www.orthodoxartsjournal.org/mercy-on-the-right-rigor-on-the-left/, accessed 27th September 2016.

[48] Cited in Jonathan Pageau, 'Mercy on the Right. Rigor on the Left'.

[49] Marcus Borg, *Meeting Jesus Again for the First Time* (New York: Harper Collins Publishers, 1994), p.124.

[50] N. T. Wright, *Jesus and the Victory of God* (London: SPCK, 1996), pp.126-127.

Chapter 7
The thieves and the shadow

On the night of Friday 16th September 2011, in Canterbury Cathedral, the then Archbishop of Canterbury Dr Rowan Williams entered into dialogue with the comedian Frank Skinner. During that discussion, Dr Williams told this story:

> I remember when I was a teenager, a priest in our parish telling me that he had come to talk to the Mother's Union about Jesus, and said, 'We have to remember that Jesus was a real human being and he had dusty feet.'
>
> 'Yes,' they all nodded.
>
> He went on, 'And he had dirty feet.'
>
> Slight intake of breath.
>
> 'He even had… smelly feet.'
>
> And that was the point at which his job was on the line.

In a similar fashion, many devout Roman Catholics were a little shocked to hear the words of Pope Francis when he preached a sermon on the account in St Luke's Gospel of the boy Jesus remaining in Jerusalem to discuss with the teachers while the rest of the holy family returned home. He said, 'For this little escapade Jesus probably had to ask forgiveness of his parents. The gospel doesn't say this but I believe we can presume it.'

For one contributor to the paper *The Remnant*, the title of his comments to Pope Francis' sermon just about sums up the concerns: 'Even God needs Mercy. A troubling Homily by Pope Francis.'[51] Troubling indeed! To ask for forgiveness presumes the committing of sin, and that is *not* something that Jesus, who was most *definitely without* sin, had to do.

Both stories show the delicate balance between affirming the full humanity of Jesus while adhering to doctrine and to Scripture:

Therefore he had to be made like his brethren in every respect, so that he might become a merciful and faithful high priest in the service of God.
Hebrews 2:17

And later in the Epistle to the Hebrews:

Since then we have a great high priest who has passed through the heavens, Jesus, the Son of God, let us hold fast our confession. For we have not a high priest who is unable to sympathize with our weaknesses, but one who in every respect has been tempted as we are, yet without sin.
Hebrews 4:14-15

And again, as St Paul reminds his readers:

For our sake he made him to be sin who knew no sin, so that in him we might become the righteousness of God.
2 Corinthians 5:21

The balance between maintaining the true humanity of Jesus with His divinity is also to revisit the fourth-century argument between Apollinarius of Laodicea and one of the Cappadocian Fathers, Gregory of Nazianzus. Apollinarius agreed that Jesus was truly human in the flesh, but believed that He did not have a human mind – it only *seemed* to be human. Gregory responded with the well-known words, 'What has not been assumed has not been healed,' or, to put it more bluntly, 'What use to us is Jesus if he was only human from the neck down (so to speak), if he did not assume a human mind?'[52]

In this chapter, the difficult and no doubt controversial question will be asked and then explored: 'Did Jesus have a shadow side?' It must be stated from the outset that this question will be tackled firmly within the framework of the *sinlessness* of Jesus and the scriptural/doctrinal claim that Jesus in His humanity was like us in *every* respect, which must include a full appreciation of both the physical and the psychological. And it must be emphasised that it is a question which will be answered in different ways.

But why should a question such as this be asked at all? Firstly, it is in keeping with St Luke's Gospel, particularly in the deep understanding that he consistently shows concerning the inner lives, the damaged souls, which find healing grace in the presence of Jesus. This is not surprising, for St Paul writes at the end of his Epistle to the Colossians of the presence of the 'beloved physician' Luke (Colossians 4:14). The original Greek here is most illuminating for the question of this chapter and for the continuity of the book as a whole, for the word translated as 'physician' is *iatros*, and establishing that St Luke had a keen understanding of the condition of a person's soul, or in Greek, *psyche*, it can be argued that St Luke could be termed a doctor of the soul, a *psyche iatros*, in essence a *psychiatrist*.

Secondly, there is implicit within the question a pastoral imperative. Knowing that Jesus understood in every respect the struggles of all humanity, including the mental struggles, is a sign of immense hope to those who have to face these challenges on a daily basis. Again, this is not without scriptural evidence. The incident is the healing of the boy with epilepsy/demon possession (Matthew 17:14-21; Mark 9:14-29; Luke 9:37-43). Reeves writes:

> The Greek of Matthew's text gives an indication of the torment of those with mental illness, which was recognised by the author as being something close to the personal suffering of Christ himself. This is what John Nolland says about the language used by Matthew in verse 17:
>
> 'With one exception, Matthew uses *kakaos* [lit. 'badly'] exclusively with reference to the sufferings of those cured by Jesus. The idiom is normally *kakos ekein* [lit. 'have badly'], but here it is the stronger *kakos pasxien* ['suffer badly'] using a verb normally reserved for the sufferings of Jesus.'[53]
>
> What Matthew seems to be saying is that those who suffer and manifest mental torment … have a particular 'Christ-likeness' about them.[54]

So with the various scriptural and doctrinal safeguards in place, how this question will be explored will require moving between the disciplines of psychology and theology, and will use the objective presence of the thieves either side of Jesus as subjective psychological voices during His tortuous suffering.

The idea of the 'shadow side' is a term coined and explored at length by the analytical psychologist Carl Jung, and it is his work in this area of human experience that the question of the shadow side of Jesus to which this chapter will refer (in, it must be emphasised, an amateur way). Why should such a question be asked? It comes back to the understanding that Jesus was human in every way that we are human, and yet He was without sin. But what is this shadow?

It isn't to be confused with being evil or even being sinful. If it was, it is certainly a question that *couldn't* be asked of Jesus. But, given the right conditions and a free rein, it can *tend* towards that state, in the same way that being tempted is not a sin in itself but giving in to the temptation is. Simply put, the shadow side is that part of being human – certain behaviour, attitude, aspects of humanity – that have been driven back into the unconscious.

Jung was convinced that everybody carried a shadow side, and the less it was part of an individual's consciousness, the darker and denser it was likely to be. But if a particular inferiority was in the conscious mind, there would be every opportunity to be able to correct it. Furthermore, it would be in contact with more healthy aspects and interests which could be used to continually modify that presentation of the shadow. However, the more an aspect of the shadow is ignored and suppressed and pushed into the unconscious, the less chance it has to be corrected, and the more shameful aspects, the deviant and the twisted, are hidden and ignored. Hidden so that others are not subjected to them, as the more palatable and likeable characteristics are paraded in order to ensure a degree of likeability and attractiveness.

This attractive side Jung called the 'ego-ideal', the 'persona', the bit of our character that rejects all those elements that are part of the shadow. As this is the opposite pole, there now exists a shadow – persona polarity. So, for example, the person who is all persona would equate to the perfectionist, who hides and buries his shadow – all the weaknesses and bad stuff – for fear of failure. This requires a great deal of energy and effort, and when the shadow side does break through, breakdown can often be the result. Something similar to this position can be seen in the character of Yakov Petrovich Golyadkin in Fyodor Dostoyevsky's book *The Double*. Golyadkin is a tender, shy and awkward character who dreams of having great popularity, but he finds himself being pursued by someone identical to him, who even has the same name as him. But there is a difference: this Golyadkin Junior is popular and liked and confident, and he gradually takes over Golyadkin Senior's work, social circle and entire life. There comes a moment when Golyadkin Senior writes his doppelganger a note:

> Dear Yakov Petrovich, It's either you or me, but there's no room for both of us! I'm telling you quite frankly that your strange, absurd and at the same time impossible desire to appear as my twin and pass yourself off as such will serve no other purpose than to bring about your complete disgrace and defeat.[55]

The story ends with Golyadkin Senior going mad and being taken away by horse and cart to an asylum.

In another story, the fairy tale 'The Shadow' by Hans Christian Anderson, the narrative shows that each human being has a shadow that, if allowed to take over, will eventually be the cause of their destruction. This, then, is the polar opposite to the one who is all 'persona': the one who becomes all shadow, the one who obeys and adopts all kinds of deviant behaviour and gives free rein to their desires. The classic narrative that describes that particular state is Robert Louis Stevenson's *The Strange Case of Dr Jekyll and Mr Hyde*.

From a Jungian perspective, Dr Jekyll's fundamental mistake is his recklessness in giving consent to become his shadow, and in the end he reaches the point of no return.

The ideal, of course, is the state of achieving harmonisation, of reconciling both poles and integrating both the shadow and the ego-ideal so they no longer contradict within the person and cause a spiritual blockage, but are brought together creatively with the result of a far greater opportunity for spiritual growth and development. This is achieved, according to Jung, by the abandonment of 'self' with a small 's' to the authority of the true 'Self' with a capital 'S', which he called the *Imago Dei*, the image of God, in which we are all made. It is the turning towards God that harmonises the opposites, and from out of the integration of the ego-ideal and the shadow comes the potential for vitality and creativity, health and holiness.

To use a crude analogy, consider the question, 'What makes a particularly good photograph or a beautiful painting?' If there is too much shadow or the colours are too dark, the picture loses a degree of sharpness and detail. If there is no shadow, the picture becomes two-dimensional and lacks depth. But in the hands of a skilled craftsman, the picture that has the right amount of light and shadow is a picture that qualifies as perfect. The perfect harmonisation achieved by Jesus is to be in the presence of the perfect image.

The writer and Priest Henri Nouwen reflects upon the shadow side in a number of his writings that are concerned with spiritual growth. In his book *Intimacy* he says this:

> It is very difficult for each of us to believe in Christ's words, 'I did not come to call the virtuous, but sinners …' Perhaps no psychologist has stressed the need of self-acceptance as the way to self-realisation so much as Carl Jung. For Jung, self-realisation meant the integration of the shadow. It is the growing ability to allow the dark side of our personality to enter into our awareness and thus prevent a one-sided life in which only that which is presentable to the outside world is considered a real part of ourselves. To come to an inner unity, totality and wholeness, every part of our self should be accepted and integrated. Christ represents the light in us. But Christ was crucified between two murderers and we cannot deny them, and certainly not the murderers who live in us.[56]

Nouwen picks up on three important points in this statement: the problem of living a one-sided life with no acknowledgement of the opposite pole; the importance of integrating our opposites; and, of course, the inclusion of the thieves as an immediate choice for the context for this discussion.

A previous chapter made note of the literary use of the thieves as opposites alongside other people in St Luke's Gospel who occupied similar roles. On this point, and consistent with the theme of this chapter, the Benedictine monk Anselm Grun makes this observation. It is a long quote but worth stating:

> In his ideas of what a healthy life is, Luke is indebted to the Greek view of human nature. The Greeks thought that everything should be in moderation. The Greek idea of the beautiful and good person (Greek kalos kagathos) is an expression of this. Having everything in moderation involves balancing opposites. The basic question for the Greeks was how human beings could find their true natures, how they could overcome their inner divisions and find unity with themselves and God. Balancing opposites is a way to achieve this unity. So Luke is fond of including opposites in his account. When he describes one pole of human life, the opposite pole immediately follows. That is evident from the way in which he always puts a woman alongside a man as in the case of Simeon and Anna or Simon of Cyrene and the weeping women … He always describes two human poles. Both poles are part of us … in this way he preserves us from a one sided idealism in which we are always in danger of leaping to the opposite pole and thus splitting off important areas of our soul. Luke shows us a balanced way towards becoming human. He teaches us the art of living a full life by consciously perceiving and accepting the polarity of our existence.[57]

So if it can be argued that Jesus did have a shadow side, a fully integrated shadow side, and if the thieves can help to answer this question, then there is a basis for understanding and transforming our own shadow and for growing more in the likeness of Jesus; or – to use the words of St Paul – 'We have the mind of Christ' (1 Corinthians 2:16). This will be determined by certain moments in the life and ministry of Jesus as presented by Scripture, and by taking a certain degree of speculative licence with the thieves, not just as those who physically accompany Jesus at the cross, but as representatives of the psychological battle in the mind of Jesus as He battles with pain and suffering. And this can be done by way of a technique much beloved of the classic cartoon animator.

Consider the principal character in a cartoon who is faced with a moral choice. On the one hand the choice will result in something good and creative, something altruistic, but it might result in the character losing out or making a sacrifice. And on the other hand, the choice might mean something bad or negative and selfish, something more tempting and alluring that might result in some temporary personal gain but at odds with what is right. In this scenario, the cartoon character is seen to be aided in his decision-making by the appearance of an angel on his right shoulder and a devil on his left, each prompting the character to either do the right action and therefore what is good, or the bad action and what is bad.

Each protagonist, the angel and the devil, gives substance and voice to the internal dialogue that we all face when making a difficult or moral choice. To make the imaginary leap of depicting the thieves in these roles isn't that difficult when it has already been shown in a previous chapter the iconographical presence of an angel above the repentant thief, almost parallel with Jesus' right shoulder, and a devil above the unrepentant thief, again almost parallel with Jesus' left shoulder (Plate 4). Taking evidence from Scripture first, there certainly do appear to be moments where aspects of the shadow breaks through, the obvious moment being the occasion of Jesus' temptations in the desert. Concerning this, Peter Mullen writes:

> There are varieties of opinions about what actually happened at the temptations in the wilderness. Some interpreters take a literal line and picture Satan as an actual character met by Jesus face to face. Others imagine that the story of the temptation is about something that took place in Jesus' mind, a tremendous struggle out of which he emerged victorious. Whichever interpretation is preferred I think it is vital to establish one fact straight away: it must have been possible for Jesus to have given in to the temptation or else the whole episode was a sham. ... But if there was never any chance that he would lose that battle with the tempter then he was certainly not tempted as we are tempted. And that of course makes a pretence of the whole doctrine of the incarnation; for it presents us with a Jesus who was only under the appearance of a man. Essential for the doctrine of the atonement as well as that of the incarnation, is the vision of Jesus as a real man among men.[58]

This is not an isolated case, of course. There is also the anger displayed during the cleansing of the Temple, the struggle in the garden of Gethsemane, Jesus' impatience

Plate 4 Details from a fourteenth-century Crucifixion frontal by Jacopo di Cione

with the disciples, and the no-nonsense confrontations with the Scribes and the Pharisees. In all these moments the shadow side is discernible, but the outcome of each episode results in a situation that is more creative and revelatory, a clear indication that when there is true harmonisation of the opposites something transforming happens.

Looking again at the temptation narrative, and assuming for now that the tempter's voice was the voice of Jesus' shadow side, not only was it recognised and acknowledged, it was also fully grasped and integrated, resulting in the situation being transformed and harmonised. What could have resulted in a descent into a moment of self-serving, of personal power and popular celebrity, or of fear, timidity and ineffectiveness, was turned into a positive and affirming action which serves God and God alone.

Some biblical commentators have speculated on the outcome of the temptation in the wilderness were Jesus to have succumbed to all or part of all that was put before Him, if He had allowed the shadow side any leverage. John Pridmore thinks it would have brought His vocation as the anointed one to an end. He writes:

> Had Jesus have chosen the alternative path proposed by his adversary he would no doubt have still gone on to do a lot of good, but love's last battle, God's campaign to bring us home to himself, would already have been lost.[59]

To speculate further, if Jesus had succumbed to His shadow side, it could also have resulted in Jesus continuing with a messianic vocation but along the hoped-for ways that many of the Jewish people had waited for – i.e. a revolutionary Messiah, an insurrectionist, or a Barabbas-type figure. Or, to adopt the opposite state, if Jesus had shrivelled from His shadow side and not integrated it, this may have resulted in Jesus being an ineffective figure, more meek and mild, setting His face more towards the safety of the carpenter's shop than the challenges of Jerusalem.

With all speculation aside, what Scripture does give us is a fully integrated, psychologically harmonised and fully balanced man, who is also fully God and who is neither a meek and mild wilting flower nor an angry, self-serving revolutionary. The creative and clear outcome of this perfect balance allows all people who come into Jesus' orbit, allows creation itself, to reach a harmony of being. Full integration of the shadow side allows that which tends towards the destructive to become constructive. Non-integration, on the other hand, diminishes the opportunity to see constructive outcomes and settles for imbalance and dis-ease.

One shadow side, two responses

Let us turn now to the two thieves, firstly as historical characters grounded in the events of the crucifixion in first-century Jerusalem. To what extent can their shadow sides be observed from the few words that are uttered by each party? Do they give a hint of integration and therefore certain constructiveness, or do they give a glimpse of the darkness that refuses to be faced?

It is reasonable to suggest that up to this point in their lives they have both lived according to the impulses and drives of their shadows as dominant personal features. Unlike Jesus, they are not there because they are innocent; they are there because they have lived their lives favouring this shadow side and obeying its impulses. As the psychologist John Monbourquette says, 'consenting to become your shadow condemns you to a life controlled by your passions'.[60]

In the case of the impenitent thief, St Luke informs his readers that he first hurls insults at Jesus. This is immediately revealing, for in shadow therapy the classic symptom of not welcoming or integrating the shadow is to project it on to others because it cannot be personally accepted. We are not told what the insults are, but it seems reasonable to suggest that they were unconscious self-loathing and self-hatred that found a voice and thus became projected on to Jesus. His caustic question, 'Are you not the Christ?' may be an indication of the thief's revolutionary tendencies, demanding action that was often associated with a messianic military figure. Action that would be characterised by bloodshed and uprising, particularly against the occupying forces.

The words of the repentant thief and the psychological profile behind them suggest a very different mind in process. Here the words indicate shadow integration which results in an honest assessment of the thief's life, a creative request and a fruitful outcome. In all, and in a very short space, the reader is witnessing the growth into a mature spiritual response.

The penitent thief begins with his focus away from himself. He focuses on God in the person of Jesus. The thief gives voice to the fact that concerning himself, he is not the centre of the universe, but places his needs within a higher point of reference. Then we notice how he acknowledges his faults: 'We are getting what our deeds deserve; we are being punished justly.' To quote Peter Mullen again:

> The man who successfully integrates the dark side of his nature is likely to be the sort of man who has a cheerful awareness of his faults and weaknesses … He is neither morally paralysed nor under the false apprehension that he is capable of more good than a limited amount. He sees himself neither as a chief of sinners nor as angel of light. He knows his limitations. He avoids projection.[61]

Of course, it must be stressed that this observation of Mullen is applicable to humanity in its fallen nature who are growing towards being like Jesus, and is not applicable to Jesus, whose only limitations, even if such a word could be used, were the limits of an incarnated state.

The creative outcome of the thief harmonising his shadow side is to make the impossible possible and unimaginable imaginable: 'Remember me when you come into your kingdom.'

'Truly I say to you, today you will be with me in Paradise.'

Working with his shadow, the penitent thief turns a situation of personal and even maybe eternal destruction into a moment that allows the grace of God to be utterly transforming and salvific. The thief, when he comes to terms with and recognises his shadow, works with it and fully integrates it; he steals the Kingdom of heaven.

The thieves as 'types' of Christ's shadow

From the historical context, as real people who were really crucified alongside Jesus, what happens when we now place them as voices depicting the internal psychological battle that Jesus experiences while He dies slowly on the cross, carrying the sins of all humanity? The cross is the fulfilling of Jesus' vocation, and to use the language of the fourth Gospel – that of St John – this is Jesus' 'hour'. And in this final hour when Jesus accomplishes His vocation, He hears again the tempter's voice, that voice of His shadow attempting to draw Him away from His calling: 'Are you not the Christ? Save yourself!' Just like the seductive, tempting voice in the wilderness, how easy it would have been to succumb to the promptings of the shadow, to listen to the devilish voice sitting on His shoulder spitting his venom into Jesus' ear, to have called on His servants and the power of the Kingdom, and to have descended from the cross. How easy it would have been for Jesus to have put a stop to all of this in the garden of Gethsemane, that other place of wrestling with the shadow, when He announced that He could call upon His Father and have 12 legions of angels at His disposal (Matthew 26:52-55).

'Are you not the Christ? Save yourself!' This is the final assault; the final coming to terms with what being the Son of God is all about, and has been all about from the beginning of time itself. And with it comes one final opportunity to say 'no'. With few on His side, alone, facing injustice, betrayed, denied, in pain, with a sense of God's absence, an apparent failure: the perfect conditions to give free rein to the shadow. But there, alongside the tempter's voice, is another voice, the voice of a ministering angel, the words uttered by the penitent thief.

This voice calls Jesus back to His vocation, reminding Him of God's justice, reminding Him that He is totally innocent, pure and spotless. This voice calls Him back to the Kingdom of His Father, whence He came, with the task of salvation accomplished, for He doesn't go back alone; He goes back with sinful man restored, with the penitent thief by His side. The desire and temptation to listen to His shadow and save Himself is integrated, harmonised and transformed, and the result is the salvation of the thief, of all humanity, and, at the last, the whole of creation.

A few cautionary points

To end this chapter, a few cautionary notes should be added. Firstly, the temptation to act out of the darkest recesses of the shadow, the consequence of not moving on from the acknowledgement of the shadow and dealing with it, but letting it loose, can render evil as purely subjective. This in turn can lead to the false claim that the adversary, the devil, is purely a construct of the psyche. Both Scripture and experience show that the devil and his minions cannot be reduced to just processes of the mind, and that there is indeed one who prowls around looking for someone to devour (1 Peter 5:8). Equally, there is the similar trap of seeing the devil at work everywhere and demonising everything, making the devil the cause of every negative action, and claiming no personal responsibility for wrongdoing.

Secondly, the pitfall of using categories of 'opposites' (good/bad, penitent/impenitent, saved/damned) and 'the devil' in an argument such as this is to tend towards dualistic thinking. The spectre of dualistic thought has hung over much of this discussion, but what is seen in Jesus is not only a fully integrated, whole person that is capable of holding opposites together in a creative redemptive tension, but also the cross itself is a tangible symbol of reconciling opposites in an inclusive way. The vertical and horizontal aspects of the cross meet at the point where the love of God in Jesus balances the extremes: the good and the bad, the penitent and the impenitent. The holiness of Jesus enables the dualistic mind to see the majesty of God, the greatness of God as a universal, totally authoritative constant. The depth of Jesus' holiness holds the most extreme of opposites together: good/evil, light/darkness, life/death and descent into hell/ascent into heaven. Immersing oneself into the life of Jesus, growing into His likeness, into the full stature of God made flesh, enables one to confront dualistic thought in all its manifestations. Right belief does not settle with the absolutes of one-sidedness, but wrestles with the complexities of finding paradoxes in situations of seeming contradictions.

[51] Fr Brian Harrison, 'A Troubling Homily by Pope Francis', *The Remnant*, 2015.

[52] John Sweet, *Docetism: Is Jesus Christ really human or did he just appear to be so?* cited in Ben Quash and Michael Ward, *Heresies and How to Avoid Them* (London: SPCK, 2007), pp.27-28.

[53] John Nolland, *The New International Greek Testament Commentary: The Gospel of Matthew* (Michigan: Wm B. Eerdmans, 2005), p.711 (brackets as original).

[54] Graham Reeves, *Before Them Set Thy Holy Will. Iconography and Pastoral Care of Those with Mental Illness* (Cambridge: Melrose Books, 2011), pp.4-5.

[55] Fyodor Dostoyevsky, *The Double* (London Penguin, 1846), p.109.

[56] Henri Nouwen, *Intimacy*, cited in Michael Ford (ed), *The Dance of Life: Spiritual Direction with Henri Nouwen* (London: Darton Longman and Todd, 2005) p.9.

[57] Anselm Grun, *Jesus: The Image of Humanity. Luke's Account* (London: Continuum, 2003), pp.11-12.

[58] Peter Mullen, *Being Saved* (London: SCM Press, 1985), p.28.

[59] John Pridmore, *The Word is Very Near You: Sundays Year C* (Norwich: Canterbury Press, 2009), pp.87-88.

[60] John Monbourquette, *How to Befriend Your Shadow: Welcoming Your Unloved Side* (London: Darton Longman and Todd, 2001), p.57.

[61] Peter Mullen, *Being Saved*, pp.36-37.

Chapter 8
The thieves and liturgy

Right worship reveals what the Christian truly believes and is the sure witness of the defining truths of the Christian faith. *Lex orandi, Lex credendi* – the law of praying is the law of believing. How the Christian worships, the words used, the actions, the symbols, even the space where worship takes place, all speak of the relationship that the worshipper has with God and with fellow believers. Right worship gives to the gathered community of faith the guarantee that what is offered and received is the clearest expression of the truth as it has been received, to enable them to live lives worthy of bearing the name of Christ and to make that name known in Christian mission. So how does liturgy handle the scriptural texts of the two thieves, and how does participation in worship direct and form the way believers understand their roles?

As one would expect, the crucifixion narrative predominantly appears during Great Holy Week and Good Friday and is chiefly put before the worshipper in the form of the Passion reading. In the Common three-year Lectionary, the thieves form part of each of the synoptic accounts at the Eucharist on Palm Sunday, with St Matthew's account being read in Year A, St Mark's in Year

B and St Luke's, with the additional words of the thieves, in Year C. In the Tridentine Rite, St Matthew's account of the Passion is read on Palm Sunday, St Mark's Passion on Holy Tuesday and St Luke's on Holy Wednesday. In the Common Lectionary and the Tridentine Rite, the Passion for Good Friday is taken from the Gospel of St John. The extended version of St Luke's crucifixion narrative appears again at the end of Year C on the feast of Christ the King.

Opportunities for preaching specifically on the influence of the thieves for the purpose of spiritual growth seem rather arbitrary. As bit players in the crucifixion story and the Passion reading, they run the risk of remaining so unless the opportunity is firmly grasped to make something more of their association with the crucified Jesus. This occasionally happens during some Good Friday services in church communities that opt for a service based around something like the last seven sayings of Jesus from the cross, and then maybe mention of the thieves is limited to the words of Jesus: 'Truly I say to you, today you will be with me in Paradise.' (And maybe, 'Father, forgive them; for they know not what they do.') A cursory look at the material designed for liturgical services of this kind (commentaries, sermon reflections, Bible notes) finds that they follow the standard pattern of proclaiming the merits and graces bestowed on the penitent thief and the example of his insight into the true nature of the crucified Jesus, while using the impenitent thief as the prime example of the attitude that is likely to render one damned. Few, it seems, if any, dare to want to grapple with the impenitent thief theologically, although as stated at the beginning of this book, John Pridmore, in his reflective notes on the

Sunday readings, dangles this particular theological challenge for Palm Sunday in St Luke's year when he says of the penitent thief, 'Heaven is promised to the undeserving.' But then he adds in reference to the impenitent thief, 'But just a moment. There is someone else there still less deserving.'

A fascinating observation is given by Metropolitan Anthony of Sourozh concerning the Russian Orthodox liturgy of Good Friday Matins. In a footnote to his main text he comments on the service where the death of Christ is told in 12 Gospel readings interspersed with elaborate singing of antiphons and their beautiful musical settings. In particular, he singles out the *Exapostilarion*, 'A hymn read or sung towards the end of Matins is for this service a reflection on the good thief and is a well-known and loved musical piece.'[62] However, in the main body of the text, Metropolitan Anthony laments the use of such beauty because it anaesthetises the worshipper from the sheer horror of what is going on. He says:

> ... whereas to witness the killing of a living man is something quite different. That remains like a wound in the soul that one does not forget: once having seen that, one can never return to one's previous condition. And this is what frightens me – in some sense the beauty and depth of our service should be opened up; we should tear a hole through it and take every believer through that hole to the terror and majesty of what is taking place.[63]

Homilies, reflections and meditations do indeed stun the reader/hearer into the sheer utter beauty of unmerited grace of salvation, particularly in one such as the thief who came to repentance and belief, and maybe that is ultimately one of the primary goals of giving a little more liturgical space to the impenitent thief, in order to show a clear reflection of what humanity is like and is capable of being. Being exposed to the horror of this may indeed have the result of turning a few away from those conditions that resemble this thief with a vow never to return that way again.

A particular liturgical practice where the thieves are occasionally referenced in prayerful contemplation is the discipline of the Stations of the Cross. The eleventh station, 'Jesus is nailed to the cross', gives every opportunity to make the presence of the thieves part of the prayer, contemplation and meditation that draws the participants into this most sacred of moments. For the most part, the singular emphasis is on the moment Jesus is nailed and raised on the cross; however, some meditations do indeed include Jesus in the company of the thieves.

One children's meditation entitled 'A Journey with Jesus' devotes the entire eleventh station to 'Dismas, the Thief Who Was Sorry',[64] and the meditation focuses on the hope of heaven, although no mention is made of the impenitent thief, which does seem to be the case for most of the meditations available.

One meditation that does make prayerful mention of both thieves is that of the Roman Catholic priest Father Quinlan. After the Scripture passage which is St John's account of the crucifixion of Jesus with the thieves, the following prayer is said:

Almighty and eternal God, ruling the living and the dead alike, show love and mercy to all whom we have in mind during this prayer, whether this world still holds them in the flesh, or the next has already received them.[65]

Alongside this prayer both priest and people are then invited to pray:

Draw us all to yourself, for you are the One by whom alone we may enter Heaven. Have mercy also on the souls in purgatory for your bitter passion, we beseech you, and for your glorious name, Jesus.[66]

Given that this prayer is specifically in the context of the thieves, of those still 'in the flesh' (presumably referring to the impenitent thief), and for those whom heaven has 'already received' (the penitent thief), then it seems that the corresponding prayer of 'purgatory' and 'Heaven' at least allows the possibility that all hope is not entirely lost for the thief still 'in the flesh'.

One of the Church of England Liturgical books, *Times and Seasons*, also includes a set of Stations of the Cross within the Lent section. There, the eleventh station begins with the reading of the thieves from Luke 23:39-43, and although a personal meditation is suggested, the prayer that follows singles out the penitent thief and designates Jesus as 'the hope of the hopeless'.[67]

By the very nature of the relationship of the penitent thief with Jesus, the church by the year 400 CE began speaking of the thief as a saint, and although not formally canonised by the Church, Dismas was being referred to in such terms by reason of the promise made to him by Jesus

Plate 5 St Dismas, Russian Icon, Vladimir Region (St Isaac of Syria, Skete)

(Plate 5). The date set in the Sanctorale was 25th March (also the feast of the Annunciation), which, falling in the season of Lent as it does, gives every opportunity to draw into a Lenten observance the importance of true repentance after the example of the thief. A specific feast day for the penitent thief also gives the opportunity to bring before God his intercessions for those under his patronage, especially prisoners, reformed thieves and those on death row (undertakers join the list as well). Because of the association of St Dismas with prisoners, several prison ministries also operate under his patronage.

Joining the sacred ranks of those raised to the altar, St Dismas appears in at least one litany: that of St Francis De Sales in his classic work *Introduction to the Devout Life*. In his 'Second Part of the Introduction' concerning the elevation of the soul to God, St Francis writes:

> You would do well also to invoke your good Angel, and the holy persons who are concerned in the mystery upon which you are meditating: as in that of the death of our Lord, you may invoke our Lady, St John, St Mary Magdalen and *the good thief*, in order that the interior sentiments and movements which they received may be communicated to you.[68]

A rather unorthodox use of invoking the prayers of the penitent thief is given in the true story of Father Emil Kapuan:

> In November 1950, during the Korean War, North Koreans captured twelve hundred American troops. Among the prisoners was Fr Emil Kapuan, a chaplain from Pilsen, Kansas. In the POW camp, the North Koreans kept their American prisoners on starvation rations, so Father Kapuan took to stealing food from the guards' storeroom. Each night before he crept out of the

barracks on a pilfering expedition, Father Kapuan always invoked St Dismas, the good thief.[69]

Because of the universal and cosmic significance of the cross, iconographers frequently meditate upon it as they set before the church an orthodox theological statement in paint and wood. Occasionally, an icon of the crucifixion will have the thieves as part of the theological statement, and when used privately or in divine worship this gives another opportunity for the faithful to access the mysteries of humanity's fallen nature and humanity's journey towards salvation, and as a saint, Dismas features in icons painted primarily with him as the focal point for prayer. Similarly, art can function in the same way as the plate of Jacopo di Cione's altar frontal, as considered in a previous chapter.

The thieves and prayer

Each thief, in their different ways, addresses Jesus with a petition. Both turn to Jesus and effectively offer what can be understood as a prayer. The impenitent thief hurls angry words at Jesus, the naïve, immature prayer of the 'I want' kind (although that is not all his words may amount to, as the last chapter will explain further), while the repentant thief sees something more in Jesus that brings him to open his heart in confession and true repentance in order to seek a greater communion with the Lord of Life.

Mention has been made of the relative positions of the penitent thief and Jesus as they hang on their crosses. Both iconography and art favour the body of Jesus inclined towards the penitent thief while the thief looks towards the figure of Jesus next to him. No doubt the bodily position of Jesus is in response to the penitent thief's words, his prayer, and adds a certain depth to this moment of intimate communion. Theologically, this relationship speaks of prayer in action. Rowan Williams writes:

It has been said that prayer is not primarily of getting ourselves where we can see God so much as getting ourselves where God can see us – that is, getting ourselves into the light of his presence, putting aside our defences and disguises, coming into silence and stillness so that what stands before God is not the performer, the mask, the habits of self-promotion and self-protection but the naked me.[70]

The penitent thief puts himself spiritually where he can be seen by God. He strips away the masks, the excuses, the self-delusory lies, and in repentance and humility, in fear and in hope, he makes the one request that lies at the heart of all prayer: he simply wants to remain in the presence of Jesus for all eternity. The penitent thief is the ultimate symbol of God's mercy and the principal signifier of hope for all who pray to God with an openness of heart, whatever foulness and hardness that heart has been accustomed to. We turn once again to the Orthodox Metropolitan, Anthony of Sourozh, to one of his sermons:

So often we ask ourselves and one another a very tormenting question: how can I deal with my sinful condition? What can I do? I cannot avoid committing sins … What is left for me? I am tormented. I fight like one drowning, and I see no solution …

And there was a word spoken once by a Russian staretz [a holy elder] ... he said ... 'No one can live without sin, few know how to repent in such a way that their sins are washed as white as fleece, but there is one thing we all can do. When we can neither avoid sin, nor repent truly, we can then bear the burden of sin, bear it patiently, bear it with pain, bear it without doing anything to avoid the pain and the agony of it, bear it as one would bear a cross; not Christ's cross, not the cross of true discipleship, but the cross of the thief who was crucified next to him. Didn't the thief say to his companion who was blaspheming the Lord: "We are enduring because we have committed crimes – he endures sinlessly ..." And it is to him, because he had accepted the punishment, the pain, the agony, the consequences indeed of evil he had committed, of being the man he was, that Christ said, "Thou shalt be with Me today in Paradise."'[71]

In turning towards Jesus, and in effect turning back to God, the thief's words contain echoes of the prayer that Jesus taught His disciples, the 'Our Father' that stands as the central prayer of all Christians and is the spring from which all prayers flow. It has been rightly said that the Lord's Prayer contains the fullness of the gospel, and so it should follow that if what passes between Jesus and the penitent thief is also the sum of the gospel, then the prayer given by Jesus and the words of the thief should be comparable. Taking the Lucan form of the Lord's Prayer (Luke 11:1-4), a pattern can be seen:

Father, hallowed be thy name.
'Do you not fear God?'

Thy kingdom come.

'Jesus, remember me when you come into your kingdom.'
Give us each day our daily bread;

'Truly, I say to you, today you will be with me in Paradise.'
and forgive us our sins, for we ourselves forgive every
one who is indebted to us; and lead us not into
temptation.

'You are under the same sentence of condemnation ... And
we indeed justly; for we are receiving the due reward for our
deeds; but this man has done nothing wrong.'

The words of the penitent thief, then, have the
authenticity of a sincere prayer to God, and it could be
argued that it is the purest form of prayer. It speaks of
nothing other than the need for Jesus. It is a prayer that
rises above all other prayers, it asks for nothing material, it
transcends the temporary and it sees beyond the
imperishable. This love of God and wanting to be
possessed by God is the goal of all prayer. The psalmist
wrote, 'I cry aloud to God, aloud to God, that he may hear
me. In the day of my trouble I seek the Lord' (Psalm 77:1-
2). The psalmist knew that redemption can only be
received through the one God who is greater than
anything, and in recalling the saving events of the Exodus
(there is the Exodus theme once again), the journey to the
Promised Land begins. The thief's words recall the psalm
and recall God's greatness, and God replies, 'I have come
to rescue you' (Exodus 3:8).

But what of the words of the impenitent thief? He too
addresses Jesus, certainly not with the insight and depth of
humility and contrition of the penitent thief, but it is still

cast upon the One who forever intercedes for all humanity before God.

The impenitent thief's words towards Jesus may be described as lacking in any respect or understanding, but in many ways these words are still able to offer a degree of permission to stand before God and bare one's soul when it is angry and desperate and hurting. In life's darkest hour, when there is nowhere else to turn, when all the artificial and self-preserving, self-made structures have finally proven to be inadequate, God remains, waiting for that opportunity to hear the hurt, and waiting patiently to break in when all that is left is breakdown.

The thief raises his voice at heaven and metaphorically clenches his fist at the Saviour and Redeemer. He is not the first or the last to do this in human history out of sheer frustration at the apparent silence and inactivity of God. The thief gives permission to all who experience hopeless and shameful situations to present their emotionally charged prayers to God. Releasing anger towards God in prayer is not wrong, particularly when it can be used as a means of developing a deeper understanding of our relationship with God and the activity of God. Censuring one's prayers, hiding anger and disturbing thoughts, is a false exercise, considering that God knows the deepest workings of each heart better than each person knows their own. Pierre Wolff writes:

> Anger and hatred which separate us from God and others, can also become the doorway to greater intimacy with God. Religious and secular taboos against expressing negative emotions evoke shame and guilt. Only by expressing our anger and resentment

directly to God in prayer will we come to know the fullness of love and freedom. Only in pouring out our story of fear, rejection, hatred and bitterness can we hoped to be healed.[72]

The tradition and discipline of praying the psalms provides an unparalleled way of giving voice to the confused, irritating and blame-seeking that beset the interior thoughts and actions of many who single God out to vent the turmoil of life. As Esther de Waal makes clear:

> The psalms allow me to face my inner conflicts. They allow me to shake my fist at God one moment, and the next to break out into spontaneous song, I am angry and then I am grateful. I complain at the bitterness of my lot, and then I rejoice at the untold blessings which I receive. If I discover the fullness of my own humanity I also discover the many faces of God.[73]

There is one indication that the impenitent thief is not just the self-absorbed, dark character that history makes him out to be, one chink in the impenetrable armour of blindness, and that is in his demand to Jesus for escape and release, for the 'salvation' he demands is not restricted to himself, but to 'us'. However he perceives salvation – and all indications would suggest some kind of immediate overturning of their current situation, a salvation from the moment rather than a salvation into eternity – his request includes his partner, the other thief. More will be said about this in the final chapter, but for now it is sufficient to point out that the impenitent thief offers *intercession*. He brings the needs of another before Jesus; he recognises his neighbour and holds him before God.

s and death

, an arena of death. A cruel spectacle where
emned to crucifixion would spend their last
hours displayed for all to see. Crucifixion was a
ic punishment, and no amount of exegesis or
on St Luke's depiction of the death of Jesus and
es can overlook or gloss over that the reader is
to and present to men dying.

r than through the media, this is not something that
porary Western culture will ever experience. Death,
erienced by most people today, is sanitised,
ised, clinicalised and mostly hidden behind
hospital or hospice doors. And when death does occur,
most cases, thanks to modern medicine and palliative care,
will be peaceful and relatively pain free. Despite the many
vain attempts that modern society tries to put in place to
stave off the process of dying and death itself, there is no
escaping it, and one day all people will take that last step,
that short walk into the known and yet unknown. St
Benedict reminds his monks in the Rule:

> Live in fear of judgement day and have a great horror
> of hell. Yearn for everlasting life with holy desire. Day
> by day remind yourself that you are going to die. Hour
> by hour keep careful watch over all you do aware that
> God's gaze is upon you wherever you may be.[74]

But how does one prepare for the day of death? How
can death be greeted as a friend rather than an enemy?
Death that comes because of natural causes or long-term
illness gives the opportunity to contemplate death and

prepare the soul for the journey. However, that is fine when there is time, but what about when death comes unexpectedly, with no warning and no time for preparation? The two thieves approach death differently, and each one can offer some clues that help towards facing death.

What is immediately apparent is the isolation and loneliness of their deaths. Jesus, the Gospels tell us, had the company of some of His followers: His Mother the Blessed Virgin Mary, and His close companion St John. There is no mention that the thieves had anyone to weep for them. Nevertheless, Jesus and the thieves had to face their own death: face it, grasp it, and take the journey by themselves. But the penitent thief doesn't make that journey on his own; he makes it with Jesus. For those who desire it, there is always the reality of having Jesus for company at the point of death, to make that last prayer for His eternal companionship and hear the words of promised life in His perpetual light. The impenitent thief occupies that same space, and although he witnesses the giving and receiving of the promise of being with Jesus, he chooses the path of isolation.

Hope, happiness and eternal life with Jesus are right in front of him and right in front of all people, but Jesus is there as a life choice, not just a death choice. The example of each thief is an echo of Moses' words before the people of Israel enter the Promised Land:

See, I have set before you this day life and good, death and evil. If you obey the commandments of the Lord your God which I command you this day, by loving the Lord your God, by walking in his ways, and by keeping

his commandments and his statutes and his ordinances, then you shall live and multiply, and the Lord your God will bless you in the land which you are entering to take possession of it.
Deuteronomy 30:15–16

The penitent thief chooses life. The impenitent thief chooses death; he chooses to stand apart from Jesus, and for want of a better word, this is hell. Rejection of every opportunity to accept life is a viable choice and is very possible, which surely makes hell a possibility too. What makes the penitent thief's response different? It is different because he lets go of everything; he lets go of life itself. 'Remember me when you come in your kingdom.' He can ask this because he has put into practice the teaching of Jesus: 'If any man would come after me, let him deny himself and take up his cross daily and follow me' (Luke 9:23), and again, 'Whoever seeks to gain his life will lose it, but whoever loses his life will preserve it' (Luke 17:33).

The penitent thief takes and accepts his cross; he follows Jesus, he loses his life and so gains eternal life. The penitent thief lets go and so faces death knowing that it is not the end. The impenitent thief cannot let go; he will not go gently into the night. The penitent thief gives the pattern and the model for the daily contemplation of death, of fear of judgement and hell, of the knowledge that all of us are under the gaze of Jesus and the constant practice of letting go into the love of God.

The thieves and salvation

The catechism of the Council of Trent on baptism states:

Should any unforeseen accident make it impossible for adults to be washed in the salutary waters, their intention and determination to receive baptism and their repentance for past sins will avail them to grace and righteousness.[75]

The revised Catechism, prepared following the Second Vatican Ecumenical Council, gives further explanation of the final state of a person who dies with Christ but before the sacrament of baptism can be administered:

Baptism is necessary for salvation for those to whom the gospel has been proclaimed and who have had the possibility of asking for this sacrament.[76]

Concerning the penitent thief, it is apparent that the exemption comes into force. The evidence before us suggests that he had no possibility of asking for the sacrament of baptism, and yet because his lips confessed that Jesus is Lord and he believed that God would raise him from the dead, then he 'will be saved' (Romans 10:9).

In a very thought-provoking exegesis of the two thieves of Luke's Gospel, Dr Peter Widdicombe sets out some of the patristic thoughts that highlighted some of the exceptions that help explain the salvation of the penitent thief in the apparent absence of baptism. Some of the exceptions put forward by the Fathers of the early church include 'those who die before they receive baptism, such as catechumen martyrs', and 'those baptised in their own blood and sanctified with a martyr's suffering'.[77]

St Augustine initially declared that the 'thief had received the Holy Spirit despite not being baptised sacramentally, for without the Spirit it would have been impossible for the thief to have said, "Remember me Lord when you come into your kingdom."'[78] The catechism of the Roman Catholic Church reflects these exceptions and lists them with a preamble that states, 'God has bound salvation to the sacrament of baptism, but he himself is not bound by his sacraments.'[79] The exceptions are:

(1258). Those who suffer death for the sake of the faith without receiving baptism are baptised by their death for and with Christ.

(1259). For catechumens who die before their baptism, their explicit desire to receive it, together with repentance for their sins … assures them of salvation that they were not able to receive through the sacrament.

(1260). Every man who is ignorant of the gospel of Christ and of his Church but seeks the truth and does the will of God in accordance with his understanding of it, can be saved.[80]

However the penitent thief's salvation was attained, there is no denying that his *desire* for union with Jesus in those last moments of his life was his primary concern. But not all are in agreement, including St Augustine, who was to change and modify his thinking, stating that it cannot be categorically proved that the penitent thief wasn't baptised. Again to quote from Dr Widdicombe's paper, St Augustine speculates, 'The thief may have been baptised by the water that gushed with blood out of Christ's side, or when the thief was in prison.'[81]

Although this is something that cannot be proven, there is an eighth-century icon from St Catherine's Monastery, Mount Sinai, entitled *The Crucifixion*, which does show the blood of the crucified Jesus falling on the head of the penitent thief in the nature of baptism (Plate 6). Concerning this icon, Sister Wendy Beckett writes, 'This noble Jesus has given all. He still holds His hands outstretched (and blood from the right hand is not wasted, it baptises the repentant thief).'[82]

This would indicate that this particular explanation of holding baptism and the thief's salvation together was part of the iconographer's meditation and understanding when painting the icon, and he saw it as a legitimate presentation of the church's faith and teaching.

These are not the only theories that have been proposed by exegetes looking for possibilities for understanding the conversion/salvation of the penitent thief. In a biblical commentary on St Luke by J. C. Ryle, he evidences some of the ways in which the conversion of the penitent thief has been portrayed by Catholic thinkers (and equally dismisses them as utter rubbish, hence the use of exclamation marks in his comments). Channels of conversion/salvation may have included:

The shadow of Christ on the cross, as the day wore on fell on the thief and was the cause of his conversion as the shadow of Peter healed the sick! ... the virgin Mary stood between the thief and Christ, and obtained grace for him![83]

Plate 6 *The Crucifixion*, eighth century

Is it so ridiculous, as J. C. Ryle would have his readers believe, that either of these two explanations carries no possibility of aiding the penitent thief towards the scales falling from his eyes and believing that Jesus is the Way, the Truth and the Life? Particularly in the possibility of the intercession of the Blessed Virgin Mary who, standing at the cross, must have felt for all three in her gentle and motherly way? After all, it is through the Blessed Mary that Jesus was given to humankind, and it seems reasonable that she would forever want to further her part in the salvation by bringing all humanity to her Son in intercession.

Three crosses

The three crosses reflect back to the world its own experience, its own reality. Each cross interprets a world that is rebellious, redeemed and renewed, and all people confront this mix and contribute to each state depending on which cross figures predominantly in thought, word and deed.

The central cross, that of Jesus, reflects sin transformed. It draws out the poison of a distorted world and reflects it back, emptied and drained of its destructive power. It does so because it is replaced by love and forgiveness, the hope of new life and a community to carry these attributes of God into the future. Standing before this cross bears witness to the clearest evidence that amid the darkness of a world turned against itself, amid every good work, every sacrifice that is thwarted and dismissed as weak, amid every act of destruction both natural and self-afflicted, the light of God's vision for all to become 'love' will break through and will not be stopped until that vision is fully complete. The cross of Jesus doesn't stop the darkness constantly trying to erupt through the fabric of God's vision, when it is given free rein and an accommodating channel, but it does give it notice that its time is limited, and that ultimately it has nowhere to go other than to consume itself or become all consumed by that which itself is all love.

This first cross presents the observer with a choice: to collaborate with the forces of sin and be a dealer in death, forever slamming the doors of the Kingdom in people's faces, or to plunge into the outstretched arms of the One who restores our humanity that we might share in His divinity and become the means by which the Kingdom is made real and accessible for all. On the subject of humanity and divinity, the one who contemplates this cross is prevented from falling into the heretical thought of giving too much weight to the humanity of Jesus, with the possibility of seeing Him as just some super human, or making Him too divine so that He just appears to be human. This cross shows the full humanity of Jesus in His suffering and death, and the full divinity of Jesus in having the authority to grant the penitent thief a place in His Father's Kingdom.

The second cross is that of the repentant thief. This cross represents a new way, a different way to live. It provides the best example of an alternative to living in a world that has lost its way. It doesn't say that God's people will be spared suffering or hardship, persecution or injustice, but it does say that alongside Jesus there is a hope that is much bigger than anything that gives the lie that we are made to face nothing but a meaningless existence and an eternity of nothingness. It is this cross that gives the contrite of heart the knowledge that all people are but dust, but this dust, although it weeps in the reality of death and mortality, goes to the grave singing 'Alleluya, Alleluya, Alleluya!' This cross is humanity's shining light through the darkness of sin. It is the point of every story, every gesture, every encounter that Jesus made. As John the Baptist pointed towards Jesus and announced that this was the One to take away the sins of the world, the thief comes at the end of a long line of people who knew this to be true; and in case anyone was still in doubt, the thief embodies this truth and displays it from the cross for all to see.

This cross ends the lie that there is an eternal battle between good and evil, for it demonstrates that as God made all things good, humanity tends to twist and warp this good until it becomes something bad and eventually sinful, but good is always there to be rediscovered, that original blessing is never taken away, and the thief shows that all people can, when they turn to Jesus, rediscover this treasure. This cross defies the accusation that somebody is all bad or, as the media like to portray, 'pure evil'. In the presence of divine mercy, godliness can be rekindled even in the face of ungodly actions. The cross of the penitent thief is a pastoral cross, for it drives home the truth that whatever is brought to God with sincerity and contrition, God can save.

The third cross, that of the impenitent thief, becomes the symbol of a world gone wrong. This cross is the reflection of the world that has rejected God, and so becomes the

tion of every act of violence, every corrupt
very relationship that seeks to domineer, bully
ss. This cross demonstrates the sad consequence
the image of God, an image in which all people
under so much that is profane that it becomes
isible. Even here, though, that image is not
d – it would be a mistake to make that claim –
eglected, so deeply buried under sin that the
connect with the fullness of God's image that
to him. This also makes it a very lonely cross.

death that ends in misery and defeat and
bitterness because this thief has been the captain of his own
soul, his own arbiter of truth and the manager of his own
destiny, and there is no room to counter this attitude with
voices of persuasive reason.

This cross refuses to listen; it is a mirror image of a
world that wishes to silence the voice of the faithful and
despises those who witness to a different way, a different
vision where the Kingdom is not a delusion but the light
by which the whole of life finds meaning. The question that
proceeds from this cross, 'Are you not the Christ?' is a
question that has already been put to Jesus during His trial.
While before the council of chief priests, scribes and elders,
Jesus is asked, 'If you are the Christ tell us' (Luke 22:66-71).

Jesus' reply reflects a sure understanding of the
situation: 'If I tell you, you will not believe.'

The cross of the impenitent thief reflects a world that
mockingly questions the person, relevance and language
of faith, with no intention of hearing or acting upon a
reasoned, truth-filled answer. The question does not
originate from a legitimate search for God; it comes from

the hardened ground of a closed mind where the seeds of the knowledge and wisdom of God are doomed to die.

This cross is also a judgement on such a world, for while Jesus responds to it with silence, it doesn't have the assurance of salvation that the second cross is granted. This is a cross that demands satisfaction and gratification now. This fits in well with a modern society that has lost the ability to wait, and even more sadly lost consciousness concerning eternity. It is a cross that always demands a miracle, the enthronement of *Chronos*, 'my time' rather than *Kairos*, 'God's time', and because it always wants the miracle, life's events are never allowed to be seen within the bigger picture of God's vision. This cross plays a dangerous and nihilistic game.

Three crosses: one the gateway to eternity, one that presents the problem of humanity, one that presents the solution to that problem.

62 Metropolitan Anthony of Sourozh, *Encounter*, p.303.

63 Ibid., p.162.

64 James Allen, *A Journey with Jesus, The Eleventh Station* (Minnesota: The Liturgical Press, 1995), p.25.

65 Fr Quinlan, *Stations of the Cross. The Eleventh Station* (England: The Catholic Printing Company, 1964).

66 Ibid.

67 The Archbishops' Council *Times and Seasons* (London: Church House Publishing, 2006), p.249.

68 Francis De Sales, *Introduction to the Devout Life* (London: Baronius Press, 2006), p.55 (emphasis mine).

69 Thomas J. Craughwell, *This Saint's for You!* (Philadelphia: Quirk Books, 2007), p.431.

70 Rowan Williams, *Tokens of Trust*, p.155.

71 Metropolitan Anthony of Sourozh, *Coming Closer to Christ: Confession and Forgiveness* (London: SPCK, 2009), pp.79-80.

72 Cited in Henri Nouwen, *Spiritual Direction* (London: SPCK, 2007), pp.59-60.

73 Esther De Waal, *Living with Contradictions* (Norwich: Canterbury Press, 2003), p.130.

74 Timothy Fry OSB, *The Rule of St Benedict in English*, p.28.

75 'The Sacrament of Baptism', The Catechism of Trent (See 'Ordinarily They Are Not Baptised At Once'). Available at cin.org/users/james/ebooks/master/trent/tsacr-b.htm (accessed 14th November 2016).

76 *Apostolic Constitution Fidei Depositum: Catechism of the Catholic Church* (London: Bloomsbury, 1994), p.285.

77 Peter Widdicombe, *The Two Thieves of Luke 23:32-43: Patristic Exegesis*, Studia Patristica XII (Oxford: Peeters Publishers, 2006) pp.273-280.

78 Ibid., pp.273-280.

79 *Apostolic Constitution Fidei Depositum: Catechism of the Catholic Church*, p.285.

80 *Apostolic Constitution Fidei Depositum: Catechism of the Catholic Church*, p.285.

81 Peter Widdicombe, *The Two Thieves of Luke 22:32-43: Patristic Thought*, pp.273-280.

82 Sr Wendy Beckett, *The Iconic Jesus* (UK: St Paul's, 2011), pp.80-83.

[83] J. C. Ryle, *Luke Vol 2* (UK: The Banner of Truth Trust, 2012), p.353.

Chapter 9
Hope for the impenitent thief?

The evidence so far shows that the impenitent thief has substituted hope in this life for one last petulant tirade, one more show of selfish anger that during his lifetime had probably enabled him to get what he desired. But the question that now remains to be answered is this: is there any hope left at all beyond this life for this man? Any chance that what he failed to realise in this life, in these last moments of life, may be realised in the next, with the opportunity to finally and voluntarily accept the truth and be drawn into the nearer presence of God? A previous chapter showed that at least one liturgical text hinted at the possibility of purgatory rather than damnation, but a single text by itself doesn't give assurance.

The church teaches that God does not predestine anyone to go to hell and makes no claim to name anyone that is in hell. What burns at the heart of God – and the cross is evidence of this – is the total desire for no one to perish, but for all to order their lives in such a way that an active choice is made to want to be with the Father. God does not choose to put anybody in hell; each person who makes that choice does so because they are free to do so.

The choice to abandon God in this lifetime will not be overruled by God in the next, and if God wished to overrule that life choice, how much more of a hell would it be for that person to be subjected to an eternity that he or she has wilfully kicked against in life? Judgement will not be something that God will hand down; judgement will be seeing ourselves, what we have truly been, including the choice to reject God, and those choices continuing to be honoured. St Augustine is said to have put it well in a simple statement that captures the very essence of the dynamic of the two thieves: 'Without God we cannot. Without us God will not.'

Even Jesus in those last moments had nothing to say to the impenitent thief. The thief was met with a resigned silence. A silence of one who knows that all that can be said has been said. There was no welcome for Jesus in this lifetime, no return of the greeting of peace, and so this silence speaks of dust being shaken off as Jesus takes His leave as a testimony against the thief.

But what if this silence is a space that effectively leaves room for another ending? What if it is a silence that leaves the story in the air, a loose end waiting for the reader to bring it to a more merciful ending? There are those who have tried, and some of these more charitable endings, whether they are arguments from theology, imagination or sentimentality, continue to give depth to an already deep scriptural text.

Before any comment is made on finding an argument that suggests that there is still hope to be had for the impenitent thief, there is one pitfall to be mindful of, and that is to turn him into someone who appears to be more deserving of God's mercy specifically because he is more outside than any of the other outsiders that St Luke talks passionately about. While it is desperately right to want the salvation of all people, it must not be at the expense of making God a moral vacuum, and must not make mercy a cheap gift to be handed out if it means nothing to the recipient. Jesus is merciful with the penitent thief precisely because he is *penitent*. Leniency is shown because this thief rent his heart, and the actions of Jesus are consistent with His message that God's mercy is always much bigger than the total amount of humanity's wrongdoing, but there are ways of being that are contrary to God's way, and there are actions that are worthy of condemnation if one remains stiff-necked and hard of heart. If there is a positive role to flow from the negative actions of the impenitent thief, it isn't to be found in looking at this thief and thanking God that 'we are not like this man', or to pile on him all the ills and evils of the world. It is to show humanity what lies beneath all people, and how that can be transformed by making the connection with the penitent thief, who in turn makes the connection with Jesus.

Speculation has already been made on the meaning that may possibly lie behind the silence of Jesus in response to the impenitent thief's anger, but at least it was just that: *silence*. There are no words of condemnation uttered by Jesus, no words that convict. The impenitent thief has been duly condemned by the authorities, and sentence is carried out under the provision of the law. The penitent thief condemns him, for he reminds his co-accused that they deserve their punishment. The group of onlookers condemn him; there is no evidence that anybody weeps for him. The one man who probably has more right than anyone to condemn him is Jesus, but He utters not a word;

He just suffers the agony of the cross and condemns the sin that put Him there, not the man who carried out the sin.

St Luke makes much more of the crucifixion of the thieves than any other Gospel writer. He also provides us with the first words that Jesus utters as He arrives at Calvary: 'Father forgive them, for they know not what they do' (Luke 23:34). As many biblical scholars point out, these words uttered by Jesus are not found in all early manuscripts, so their reliability comes under question. However, the words fall naturally off the tongue of the One who consistently showed forgiveness in His ministry, and they sit well with St Luke's Gospel as a whole.

There are three things worth noting about this prayer of Jesus in the final moments of His life, and in the context of finding eternal hope for the impenitent thief. Firstly, forgiveness seems to be particularly asked for those who are doing the actual killing, but is it also a prayer for the whole company on that grim and bloodied hill? Secondly, did the penitent thief ask to be remembered because he knew that those words of forgiveness were for him too, so he didn't need to ask to be forgiven a second time, for he grasped that offer of forgiveness and proceeded straight to ask for the Kingdom? If this is indeed the case, was the impenitent thief also forgiven but didn't grasp the enormity of that absolution until after he had died? And thirdly, Jesus asks His Father to forgive. Maybe in this moment where Jesus' humanity is under assault, He asks the Father to do for Him that which at this moment He has no power left to do. Perhaps it is just the sheer ignorance of the impenitent thief that prevents him from seeing the presence of God in the tortured and torn body of Jesus, in which case forgiveness is his because he cannot be held culpable for his ignorance; it becomes the doorway to eternity, for he knew not what he was doing.

After Jesus promised the repentant thief a place in the Kingdom, St Luke gives the hour when all this takes place: 'the sixth hour'. He then moves forward into the afternoon: 'the ninth hour', when Jesus utters his last words: 'Father, into thy hands I commit my spirit!' and the curtain in the Temple is torn in two. What happens in those three hours? Again, with nothing recorded, with no further verbal communication, no one can say how those last hours may have influenced the mind of the impenitent thief. The likelihood is that nothing much changed, but then again, in those unrecorded moments and from deep within him he may have silently put himself right with God.

What has been suggested so far applies while the impenitent thief is still alive, but what about post-mortem? Other than the hope of purgatory, does any suggestion of the hope of redemption after the moment of death become untheological? Sister Wendy Beckett doesn't seem to think so. Reference has already been made to the eighth-century *Crucifixion* icon which features the repentant thief, but describing the icon, Sister Wendy writes:

> On either side of the angels would have been sun and moon: the icon is not complete it has been injured by time. Below that, equally fragmented, would have been the two thieves, one of whom accepted Jesus, one of whom died blaspheming. The look of patient love on Jesus' face leads one to hope that both these sinners came to salvation, one while he was dying and the other in death when he saw the truth of God.[84]

Turning once again to the words of the impenitent thief, as much as history, homiletics and general opinion depict this man as a vile offender with no redeeming features, he isn't actually totally selfish. In his verbal onslaught towards Jesus, he makes his demand not only for himself but for his partner as well: 'Save yourself and us!' He indeed has a weakness, but this weakness is a concern for someone else, and this someone else, loosely speaking, is his neighbour. Could this be a weakness that also becomes a strength which God will acknowledge and draw upon? Perhaps here lies another reason for Jesus' silence. Perhaps His silence is a patient silence, a silence that marks a time of waiting until they see each other face to face when Jesus will break the silence, as He sees that his concern for his 'friend' is but a small ray of light that is buried deep in the dark, and makes him one final offer of eternal salvation.

Looking for the minutest redeeming feature that God can get hold of and work on is the subject of a story told by the journalist Andrea Tornielli in his book-length interview with Pope Francis. Calling to mind a book he read, entitled *To Every Man A Penny* by Bruce Marshall, Tornielli recounts an incident in the confessional with Father Gaston:

> [Father Gaston] invites a German soldier about to be executed to make a confession. The soldier tells the priest he has had lots of sexual adventures but that he is not sorry because he enjoyed them. Seeking to absolve him, nevertheless, the priest asks him whether he is sorry that he is not sorry and the soldier says that he is. Francis says, 'It's a good example of the lengths to which God goes to enter the heart of a man, to find that

small opening that will permit him to grant grace. He does not want anyone to be lost.'[85]

Maybe the 'us' of the impenitent thief is just the small opening that Jesus needs to lavish upon him the delights of the Kingdom.

When all is said and done, the words of the penitent thief to the impenitent thief are the only words that any of us can ever say, for all of us are under condemnation and we all justly deserve a guilty sentence. All of us are both the penitent thief and the impenitent thief, for that line between good and bad is a line that runs down the middle of every human being. Martin Buber once told a tale:

> Rabbi Bunan said to his disciples, 'everyone must have two pockets so that he can reach into the one or the other according to his needs. In the right pocket are to be the words, "for my sake the world was created," and in his left, "I am earth and ashes."'[86]

Penitent thief or impenitent thief, blessed creature or dust and ashes, the parable of the Prodigal Son, which seems to be a particular point of reference in this book, proved to be a source of immense grace for Henri Nouwen, and in a previous chapter a quote was taken from his book. It seems fitting at the end of this book to take once again this insight of Nouwen's and rewrite it with the thieves taking the place of the brothers:

> This is not a story that separates the penitent thief and the impenitent thief into good and evil. Christ only is good. He loves both the penitent thief and the impenitent thief. He runs out to meet both. He wants

both to sit at His table and participate in His joy. The impenitent thief stands back, looks at Christ's merciful gesture and cannot yet step over his anger and let Christ heal him as well.

---

[84] Sr Wendy Beckett, *The Iconic Jesus*, pp.80-83.

[85] Pope Francis, *The Name of God is Mercy* (UK: Bluebird Books, 2016), pp.30-31.

[86] Martin Buber, 'Tales of the Hasidism'. Available at www.chippit.tripod.com/tales1.html (accessed 18th November 2016).

Bibliography

Allen, James, *A Journey With Jesus, Eleventh Station*, 1995, The Liturgical Press, Minnesota.

Anthony of Sourozh, Metropolitan *Encounter*, 1999, DLT, London.

Anthony of Sourozh, Metropolitan, *Coming closer to God, Confession and Forgiveness*, 2009, SPCK, London.

The Archbishops' Council, *Times and Seasons*, 2006 Church House Publishing, London.

The Archbishops' Council, *A Time to Heal: A Contribution Towards the Ministry of Healing*, Chapter 11, 2000, Church House Publishing, London.

Apostolic Constitution Fidei Depositum, *Catechism of the Catholic Church*, 1994, Bloomsbury, London.

Beckett, Wendy (Sr), *The Iconic Jesus*, 2011, St Pauls

Borg, Marcus, *Meeting Jesus Again for the First Time*, 1994, Harper Collins Publishers, New York.

Brock, Sebastian, *Treasure House of Mysteries. Exploration of the Sacred Text Through Poetry in the Syriac Tradition*, 2012, St Vladimir's Seminary Press, New York.

Congregation for Divine Worship and the Discipline of the Sacraments, *Homiletic Directory*, 2014, CTS, London.

Craughwell, J. Thomas, *This Saint's for You!* 2007, Quirk Books, Philadelphia.

De Sales, Francis (St), *Introduction to the Devout Life*, 2006, Baronius Press, London.

De Waal, Esther, *Living with Contradictions*, 2003, Canterbury Press, Norwich.

Dostoyevsky, Fyodor, *The Double*, 1864, Penguin, London.

Elliot, J. K. (Ed), *The Apocryphal Jesus, Legends of the Early Church*, 1996, OUP, UK.

Fry, Timothy OSB, *The Rule of St Benedict in English*, 1980, The Liturgical Press, Minnesota.

Gonzalez, L. Justo, *The Story Luke Tells*, 2015, Wm. B. Eerdmans, Michigan.

Grun, Anselm, *Jesus, The Image of Humanity. Luke's Account*, 2003, Continuum London.

Harrison, Brian (Fr), *A Troubling Homily by Pope Francis*, 31st December 2015, The Remnant

Lewis, C. S., *The Great Divorce*, 1946, Harper Collins Publishers, London.

Mullen, Peter, *Being Saved*, 1985, SCM Press, London.

Monbourquette, John, *How to Befriend Your Shadow*, 2001, DLT, London.

Nolland, John, *The New International Greek Testament Commentary, The Gospel of St Matthew*, 2005, Wm B. Eerdmans Publishers, Michigan.

Nouwen, Henri, *The Return of the Prodigal Son*, 1994, DLT London.

Nouwen, Henri, *Intimacy*, cited in Ford, Michael, (Ed), *The Dance of Life*, 2005, DLT London.

Nouwen, Henri, *Spiritual Direction*, 2007, SPCK London.

Pageau, Jonathan, *Mercy on the Right, Rigor on the Left*, 2013, Orthodox Art Journal, www.orthodoxartsjournal.org/mercy-on-the-right-rigor-on-the-left/

Pontifical Council for the Promotion of the New Evangelisation, *The Parables of Mercy*, 2015, Our Sunday Visitor Publishing Division, Indiana.

Pope Benedict XVI, *In The Beginning…, 1995*, T & T Clark, London.

Pope Benedict XVI, *Jesus of Nazareth. Holy Week*, 2011, CTS, London.

Pope Francis, *The Name of God is Mercy*, 2016, Bluebird Books, UK.

Pridmore, John, *The Word is Very Near You. Sundays*, 2009, Canterbury Press, Norwich.

Pridmore, John, *The* Word is Very You. Feasts and Festivals, 2010, Canterbury Press, Norwich.

Quinlan (Fr), *Stations of the Cross. Eleventh Station*, 1964, The Catholic Printing Company, England.

Ramsey, Michael, *The Christian Priest Today*, 1972, SPCK, London.

Reeves, Graham, *Before Them Set Thy Holy Will. Iconography and Pastoral Care of Those with Mental Illness*, 2011, Melrose Books Publications, Cambridge.

Ryle, J. C., *Luke, Volume 2*, 2012, The Banner of Truth Trust, UK.

Sheen, J. Fulton, *The Cross and the Beatitudes*, 2000, Liguori/Triumph Press, Missouri.

Stead, Julian, *St Benedict, A Rule for Beginners*, 1994, New City Press, New York.

Sweet, John, Chapter 2, *Docetism: Is Jesus Christ really human or did he just appear to be so?* Cited in Quash, Ben and Ward, Michael 2007, *Heresies and How to Avoid Them. Why it Matters what Christians Believe*, SPCK, London.

Wake, William & Larder, Nathaniel, *The Apocryphal New Testament, The Gospel of Nicodemus*, 1970, Simpkin, Marshall, Hamilton, Kent & Co, London.

Whitworth, Patrick, *Gospel for the Outsider*, 2014, Sacristy Press, Durham.

Widdicombe, Peter, *The Two Thieves of Luke 23:32-43 In Patristic Exegesis*, 2006, Studia Patristica XII, Peeters Publishers, Oxford.

Williams, Rowan, *Tokens of Trust*, 2007, Canterbury Press, Norwich.

Williams, Rowan, *What is Christianity?* 2015, SPCK, London.

Wright, N. T., *Jesus and the Victory of God*, 1996, SPCK, London.

www.365Rosaries.blogspot.co.uk/2011/03/march-25-saint-dismas-good-thief.html

www.jesus-passion.com/dolorous_passion_of_our_lord_jesus_christ.htm

www.cin.org/users/james/ebooks/master/trent/index.htm